KU-256-881

THE DEVELOPMENT
OF THE
MODERN STATE
A Sociological Introduction

Gianfranco Poggi

Gianfranco Poggi is Professor of Sociology in the University of Edinburgh. After taking a degree in Law in Italy in 1956, he researched and taught in Italy and at the University of California, Berkeley, where he took a Ph.D. in Sociology in 1963. Since 1964 he has taught at the University of Edinburgh, principally in the fields of social theory and political sociology, and has lectured widely in the United Kingdom, Europe, and the USA. He is the author of *Catholic Action in Italy* (1967) and *Images of Society: Essays on the Sociological Theories of Tocqueville, Marx, and Durkheim* (1972).

QMC   311417 3

a30213 003114173b

QUEEN MARY AND WESTFIELD COLLEGE LIBRARY
Mile End Road, London E1 4NS

This item is in demand. Please return it on time.
THERE ARE HEAVY FINES FOR LATE RETURN.

Due for return	Due for return	Due for return
06 OCT 1998	27 NOV 2006	
19 JAN 2007		
25 OCT 2007		
12 NOV 2007		
09 JAN 2008		
09 JAN 2008		
30 APR 2008		
28 OCT 2008		

WITHDRAWN
FROM STOCK
QMUL LIBRARY

THE DEVELOPMENT
OF THE
MODERN STATE

A Sociological Introduction

Gianfranco Poggi

Professor of Sociology in the University of Edinburgh

Hutchinson of London

195635

Hutchinson & Co (Publishers) Ltd
3 Fitzroy Square, London W1
London Melbourne Sydney Auckland
Wellington Johannesburg

First published 1978
© 1978 by the Board of Trustees of the
Leland Stanford Junior University
Printed in the United States of America

The paperback edition of this book is sold
subject to the condition that it shall not, by
way of trade or otherwise, be lent, resold,
hired out, or otherwise circulated without the
publisher's prior consent in any form of binding or
cover other than that in which it is published and
without a similar condition including this condition
being imposed on the subsequent purchaser.

ISBN 0 09 133180 3 cased
ISBN 0 09 133181 1 paper

QUEE   ARY
COLLEGE
LIBRARY

To Tom Burns,
who deserves better

Acknowledgments

I AM grateful to my colleagues Tom Burns, Tony Giddens, David Holloway, Michael Mann, Pierangelo Schiera, and Harrison White for their comments on and criticisms of previous versions of sections of this book. Special thanks are due to Professor Janos Bak of the Department of History at the University of British Columbia for attempting to save me from my worst mistakes in Chapters 2 and 3; if in my ignorance I have at some points frustrated that attempt, I apologize to him.

On the home front, I am once more much indebted to my wife Pat and our child Maria for the invaluable assistance they have lent to my work on this book.

Contents

CONTENTS

Preface

SOCIOLOGISTS in Western countries have of late become more and more concerned with various problems relating centrally to the notion of the state. One such problem is to identify the state's basic structural features, and the range and significance of their variations over time or from country to country. Another is to understand causes, modalities, and effects of the state's apparently ever-increasing involvement in all manner of societal affairs. Still another is to assess the causes and effects of the state's policies, its relations to other institutional complexes and to various international forces and agencies.

Until very recently, such themes were mostly considered foreign, or at best peripheral, to sociology's domain. This was so for at least three reasons.[1] First, sociology had arisen in societies where an institutional distinction between the "political" and the properly "social" realm was widely taken for granted; by electing the latter as its area of concern, sociology in effect chose to ignore the political realm, which was of course centered around the state. Second, in societies like the United States and Britain, where the state and civil society were not as explicitly distinguished, sociologists had largely defined their mission as exploring the humbler, more spontaneous, down-to-earth—often hidden and unsavory— aspects of social life. Their interest was in latent as against manifest forces and processes, informal as against formal arrangements, "natural" as against "planned" institutions, the underside as against the official and conspicuous side of society. Such concerns necessarily turned their attention away from an institutional complex as visible and official as the state. Finally, in most Western countries sociology had to contend for acceptance as an academic discipline against such established and respected disciplines as political philosophy, constitutional law, and political science. When it came to defining domains, the state, being central to these other disciplines, was "off limits" to sociology.

Given this background, sociology today cannot draw from its own tradition enough of what it needs to come to grips with the problem of the state. Of the greater sociologists, only Max Weber made political phenomena, and signally the state, a central theme of his work. Yet he did not live to write his "sociology of the state"; his writings on the subject are mostly essays or were left in draft form; and most sociologists, however mistakenly, consider the typology of legitimate domination his main contribution to the sociological study of politics.[2]

Another great sociologist with strong and weighty views on the state was of course Karl Marx; and we owe much of the current literature on the state (in sociology as well as in other social sciences) to students who appeal primarily to Marx for their inspiration.[3] Though it draws at various points on Marxian insights, this book emphatically is not intended as a contribution to that literature. For one thing, the texts of Marx (and Engels) that directly address political phenomena, and the state in particular, are not that many and often deal with specific and highly contingent issues of policy; and I prefer to leave the collation of and commentary upon such texts to expert Marxologists.[4] Furthermore, the current effort to bring the Marxian "critique of political economy" to bear on the policies of contemporary Western states, valuable as it is, is of limited help to sociologists seeking in the first place an understanding of the nature and origins of the state.

Marx and Engels took such problems largely for granted; and so did and do most of their followers. Their concern is not with the state's institutional features or with political processes per se, but with how, if at all, state power affects the class struggle, capital accumulation and expansion, and the struggles over the world market. Such issues may well be weightier than those that concern us in this book. But the latter appear to me significant not only in view of the task of constructing a sociology of the state, but also in view of that of developing a radical, "debunking" critique of the uses to which state power is put today. After all, I submit, the first duty of an iconoclast is to know his icons.

The Marxists' tendency to discuss political structures only from the perspective (however enlightening in itself) of the "critique of political economy" has had some unfortunate pragmatic consequences for political movements appealing to Marx as their chief inspiration. But even leaving these aside, sociologists intending to remedy their discipline's traditional lack of concern with the state should not seek help exclusively or in the first place within the Marxian tradition. Where, then, are they to turn?

There are various alternatives, of which this book explores only one. I have chosen to discuss the main phases in the development of the modern state up to the nineteenth century, after which I have summarily considered some later changes in the relation of the state to society. My focus is exclusively on the evolution of the state's internal institutional arrangements—not on the policies of states, how those policies affect other social structures, or how they have contributed to the emergence of separate national societies. I have drawn chiefly on two bodies of literature: the history of Western political institutions and, to a lesser extent, constitutional law.

Further, I have relied almost exclusively on Continental works, and in particular on publications in German. I have favored German (and Austrian and Swiss) writers for several reasons. One is that they more frequently write in general terms and from a comparative perspective, instead of dealing exclusively with this or that individual variant of a given institutional development. Another and related reason is that German works contribute more often and more explicitly to the kind of conceptual argument that I am interested in conducting. A third reason is that in German works the history of political institutions and their juridical analysis are more often seen as interrelated.

A limitation of my approach is that it does not consider the developments in political theory and ideology that accompanied the formation of the modern state.[5] It has no room for Marsilius of Padua, Locke, or Hegel, or for the interaction between their thought and the politics of their time. That interaction is itself of the greatest historical interest, and I regret having no room for it in the conception of this book.[6]

Finally, the organization of my argument as a sequence of typological constructs puts it at variance with a properly historical account. From the continuity and diversity of the historical process are extracted a few highly abstract models, each treated as a closer approximation of the nineteenth-century constitutional state, which I consider the most mature embodiment of the "*the* modern state.*" I have chosen this approach, with its obvious liabilities, as a compromise between a full-fledged historical analysis, in which a welter of individual variants and transitional conditions would obscure the distinctiveness and unity of inspiration of each successive model, and the kind of overly generalized treatment (to be discussed briefly at the end of the first chapter) that would view the last thousand years in Western political history as the inevitable unfolding of a universal evolutionary model. Naturally, the ideal types I employ should not be treated as explanatory devices in their own right. Rather, they conceptualize changing patterns of accommodation between the contrasting interests of groups that themselves change and that constitute the ultimate protagonists of the historical process. Thus the model states I describe are introduced to make the process more intelligible; they do not themselves account for it.

My choices of theme, approach, and sources could easily be contrasted with alternatives I have forgone. I have no doubt that sociologists concerned with the state could benefit, in particular, from exploring the contributions of other disciplines, such as anthropology, economics (including the Marxian critique of political economy), and political science. But I myself have made no effort to draw on any of these disciplines. I find anthropology boring. I do not understand economics. As for political science, over the last thirty years or so it seems to me to have gone to incredible lengths in order to *forget* the state; and among those political scientists of whom this is not true, a majority are probably committed to the Marxist approach(es) that I have chosen not to adopt.

As against these alternatives, I find the history of political institutions congenial, indeed at times outright fascinating, especially the best German writings in the field. As for constitutional law, which can be quite as boring as anthropology and nearly as difficult as economics, I have learned to avoid the less rewarding writers and concentrate on those who are themselves sociologically or historically informed, and whose concern with juridical analysis aids rather than impedes their grasp of larger political structures.

Whatever this combination of emphases and aversions may in the end be worth, it should at least fill serious gaps in the interests and information of many sociologists, and at best provide a handy framework for a coherent account of the secular process by which, from beginnings in the ninth century, rule over vast Western territories came to be exercised within and by the institutional complex we call the modern state.[7] The big question for sociologists is of course that of gaining a clearer understanding of the workings of the state in contemporary societies. This small exercise is intended only as a prolegomenon to that large and difficult task.

G.P.

THE DEVELOPMENT
OF THE
MODERN STATE

CHAPTER I

Introduction: *The Business of Rule*

T HE MODERN STATE is perhaps best seen as a complex set of institutional arrangements for rule operating through the continuous and regulated activities of individuals acting as occupants of offices. The state, as the sum total of such offices, reserves to itself the business of rule over a territorially bounded society; it monopolizes, in law and as far as possible in fact, all faculties and facilities pertaining to that business. And in principle it attends exclusively to that same business, as perceived in the light of its own particular interests and rules of conduct.

But what is the business of rule? The modern state is a set of institutional arrangements for doing what? Those questions are the concern of this chapter. In its title I have used the expression "rule," as I shall do throughout the book (if rarely in this chapter), because it suitably conveys the asymmetrical nature of the social relations to which it refers, and because it points to the giving and obeying of commands as the everyday substance of those relations. An alternative and more frequent formulation of our questions employs the expressions "politics" or "political." Thus we might ask what is the nature of politics? Or, perhaps, what is political business all about?

In this chapter we shall consider two significant, and significantly different, definitions of the nature of politics. One derives from a discussion of the problem put forward in the 1950's by the American political scientist David Easton. The other was formulated in the 1920's by the redoubtable German legal theorist and right-wing political ideologist Carl Schmitt.[1]

Politics as Allocation

The two formulations differ, to begin with, in the imagery of social life that serves them as backdrop. Easton's discussion[2] projects a view of the social process as a continuous flow of diverse activities by which a limited number of valuable objects are transferred to and from interacting individuals whose primary interest is in appropriating and enjoying such objects. The objects may range from physical goods to abstractions like power and the right to deference. Further, the allocation process is not a random one. If social life is to have any pattern and continuity, the process must be to a considerable extent institutionalized. It must produce or validate the assignment to certain individuals of certain objects, disvalued as well as valued.

Let us consider three basic ways of structuring this allocation process, of making it relatively predictable and stable. One is *custom*: a universally or widely shared understanding according to which valued or disvalued things rightfully pertain to certain people or positions. ("A title on the door rates a Bigelow on the floor.") Another is *exchange*: a transaction whereby one party relinquishes a valued object to another party in return for some other valued object. ("You pays your money and you takes your choice.") A third is *command*: a mechanism by which valued objects are allocated on somebody's say-so. ("I'm the boss here.")

Easton construes the whole realm of politics as related to this last modality: allocation by command. In his view, within a given interaction context you have "politics" insofar as at least some value allocations take place otherwise than by custom or exchange. Typically, customary allocations reflect consensus among all participants, not submission to someone's individual will. Typically also, parties to an exchange are equal; they agree with rather than

2

submit to one another. Political allocations, by contrast, necessarily involve the submission of one party to another's will.

Yet since the objects in question are valued and scarce, political allocations cannot rest exclusively on someone's will. Effective allocations can take place only when commands are binding: that is, when my submission to a command does not depend on my spontaneous goodwill or indifference but is enforceable against my opposition. The giver of the command must be able to back up his say-so with sanctions, typically punishment for noncompliance rather than reward for compliance.

Politics, then, deals with the allocation and handling of a resource (the ability to issue enforceable, sanctioned commands) that in turn can be used for making further allocations of other valued objects. If politics be so understood, it follows that it is an unglamorous, mundane business, working out its allocations in bits and pieces everywhere. Yet we feel intuitively that politics is instead a significant, momentous order of social business, involving major actors and taking place at the very center of society. Easton undertakes to reconcile these views by stipulating that not just any command-based allocation can be considered political—only those that take place within relatively broad and durable social contexts with broadly defined constituencies. A father's commands, the rulings of a club's chairman, or even the decisions of a corporation's executive are not properly political. Memberships in local groupings are very often voluntary; and voluntary or not, they can often be surrendered by a disaffected member without serious loss to himself. But such groupings in turn form part of a much wider one, one in which membership cannot be easily surrendered or dispensed with.

Let us call this comprehensive grouping, which typically is territorially bounded, "society." Then Easton would apply the term "political" only to those command-based allocations whose effects are directly or indirectly valid for society as a whole. So understood, political business involves particularly visible, multifaceted,

3

demanding relations of superiority-inferiority, and it generally uses as its ultimate sanction the uniquely compelling one of physical coercion. In any case, in Easton's view politics essentially takes place *within* bounded interaction contexts, which can of course be seen as existing side by side with other such contexts. Furthermore, as we have seen, politics deals with a functional problem (allocating values among interacting units) that can in principle be dealt with in at least two other institutional ways: by custom and by exchange.

Given these theoretical alternatives, are there grounds for thinking that some value allocations must be on the basis of command? Or, to rephrase the question, is politics a necessary feature and component of social life? The answer is unquestionably yes, except perhaps in the very simplest interaction contexts. It is demonstrably clear that neither custom nor exchange, nor both together, can do all the allocating that has to be done. There are bound to be contingencies that cannot be met except by command-based allocations.

Why? Because a comprehensive and rigid body of custom, minutely allocating values, cannot by its very nature allow for the mobilization of resources, the bypassing of routines, the exploration of new lines of action, which from time to time become necessary if a society is to persist, to preserve its store of values, to patrol and maintain its boundaries with nature and with other societies. A wholly custom-controlled society can persist in the face of new contingencies only if its customs empower some members to mobilize others in response to such contingencies, to devise new routines, to choose among alternative patterns of action and have their choices accepted. But this is of course to accept the necessity of command.[3] As for exchange, Durkheim showed long ago that even the most sophisticated and flexible exchange system presupposes the existence of enforceable, policed rules.[4] In Durkheim's terms, effective contracts depend on the existence of the *institution* of contract, which itself cannot be contractual but must be bindingly established and enforced. Here again we are back to the necessity of command.

4

The argument that some allocation must take place through command (in Easton's terms, the argument for the necessity of politics) leaves open the question of the mix between the three modes of allocation, a mix that will obviously vary in different circumstances. What matters here is simply that interaction contexts beyond a certain level of complexity, duration, and size must have a mechanism of allocating at least some values on the basis of command. And it follows that society must make some permanent provisions for recourse, however intermittent, to this mechanism.

Politics as Us Against the Other

Plausible as Easton's position may seem, it remains questionable whether politics ought to be defined solely or even primarily with reference to value allocations *within* interaction contexts. Some weighty arguments to the contrary are offered by Schmitt in his provocative book *Der Begriff des politischen*.[5] In 1927, when this book was first published, Schmitt was a respected if controversial practitioner of "the theory of the state," a branch of German legal scholarship bordering on political science. His book was intended to challenge what he saw as his colleagues' maddeningly circular definition of the state as a political entity and politics as the province of the state.

Schmitt held that to define the nature of politics it was necessary to identify a distinctive realm of decisions to which the term "political" could legitimately be applied. In his view this required finding two contrasting terms that bounded the political realm in the same way the realm of ethical decisions is bounded by "good/evil," that of economic decisions by "profitable/unprofitable," or that of juridical decisions by "legal/illegal." No such pair of terms had yet been agreed on for politics, Schmitt charged, because his colleagues' liberal and humanitarian prejudices kept them from seeing the true nature of the problem.

We may pause here to compare Schmitt's basic imagery of social life with Easton's. Easton, as we have seen, envisaged a number of bounded interaction contexts, each with certain ongoing sets of relatively ordered allocation processes of which at least some, though functionally equivalent to others, were best characterized as political. To Schmitt, by contrast, social life is intrinsically disorderly and menacing. Relatively orderly interaction can be maintained only within discrete contexts or societies, each of which must first and foremost keep at bay the threat of disorder and disaster permanently posed by other, outside societies that are inimical to its interests and bent on expansion at its expense. Legal, religious, economic, scientific, and other experiences are permanent potentialities of human existence; but they can be actualized only on the condition that political activity preserve those fragile (because historically produced) boundaries that separate one society from another. Although occasional activities involve participants from more than one society, by and large orderly social life goes on within individual societies none of which is coextensive with humanity. Politics is accordingly concerned with setting and maintaining the boundaries between collectivities, and in particular with protecting each collectivity's cultural identity from outside threats.

Schmitt accordingly finds his political realm defined by the distinction "friend/foe." A collectivity's quintessential political function is to decide which other collectivities are its friends and which its foes. In the confrontation between Us and the Other,[6] we define as friends those collectivities whose own definition of all other collectivities, including Us, as friend or foe appears compatible, in the given circumstances, with our preservation as an autonomous, integral society; we define as foes those whose existence or political activity threatens our integrity or autonomy. Our integrity and autonomy are paramount concerns; for only if they are preserved can we perform such other activities as may be appropriate to the spirit of our collectivity.

But if this is so, some widely accepted approaches to political business (and to the "theory of state") are untenable, notably the equating of political business and law as preached by proponents of the *Rechtsstaat*.[7] In Schmitt's view political decisions proper bear no relationship whatever to legal rules or the distinction "legal/illegal." For law can concern itself only with decisions that are or can be standardized; and decisions between friend and foe—resulting as they do from the confrontation among independent and self-serving collectivities operating outside any encompassing system of rule—are too momentous, too unpredictable, too open-ended, to be subjected to standards.

Each properly political decision, then, is inherently a decision about an emergency, an unstable and consequence-laden situation in which rapidly apprehended necessity and expediency dictate action. Effectiveness, not legality, is what counts. If anything, politics is prior to law rather than vice versa, and legal theory must acknowledge the inherent priority of the emergency over the routine of social existence.[8]

Nor should we allow conceptual manipulation or ideological argument to confuse political decisions with other realms of decision. A foe may or may not be also a collectivity with which we cannot profitably engage in economic transactions, or one that is morally evil: no matter. The decision between friend and foe is distinctive and overriding. To deal with it properly, the political decision-maker must clear his mind of all secondary considerations (juridical, moral, economic, etc.), however significant they may be within their respective nonpolitical realms. The ultimate political decision is existential, not normative: it is a response to a condition imposed on Us by the Other.

If the Other defines Us as a foe and acts as a foe to us—never mind *why* it does—we can only reciprocate in kind. And our response must perforce entail, if not the actuality, at least the possibility, of armed conflict:

When all is said and done, the real sense of the concept of foe, of political conflict, etc., is to be found in the possibility of the actual exercise of physical violence, culminating in the physical annihilation of the foe. . . . War is but the consequent actualization of foe-ness. . . . War is not the content, the end, or the sole means of politics, but a condition whose *actual possibility* politics presupposes. The "political

7

element" lies not in war itself, which has techniques of its own, but in conduct relating to the *actual possibility* of war, in the acknowledgment of the situation it creates for the collectivity.[9]

Thus politics involves a *continuous* preparedness for possible conflict with inimical Others. Further, although politics is only one of many distinctive and mutually irreducible forms of human activity, it is intrinsically superior to all others because it is centrally concerned with preserving the collectivity without whose existence all other activities could not properly take place. Political decisions deal with the intrinsically disordered and thus menace-laden nature of the relations between collectivities. No other decisions approach them in importance.

What Easton sees as politics Schmitt would see as at best a derivative, low-grade variety of political experience. To be sure, in the course of dealing with other collectivities as friends and foes, a society will necessarily encounter some internal allocative problems. Someone will have to decree, for example, which organs will be charged with which decisions, what their powers will be, who is to man them, and how they will impinge on the distribution of which social values among individuals and groups. But woe to the collectivity that reduces its politics to these problems alone. For how is such a collectivity to decide normatively who is its foe, or deal with him by invoking rules? However it may be within collectivities, the relations between them take place in a normative vacuum; the readiness is all.

In Schmitt's view, the fact that the world is pluralistically constituted, in the sense of being made up of more than one political entity, makes it imperative that no collectivity permit any internal political pluralism, any multiplication or dispersion of the centers of political decision. Within each collectivity, only one center can have the right to make such decisions, and this right must be jealously guarded. Indeed, ultimately a single individual must make each properly political decision, since only a single mind can effectively weigh the momentous contingencies involved in deciding the paramount question of who are the collectivity's friends and foes. Normative considerations, however dear to the liberal mind, are inherently irrelevant to the desperate business at hand:

War, the fighting men's readiness to die, the physical annihilation of other men on the side of the foe—all this has no normative significance, but purely an existential one; and this lies in the reality of the actual struggle, not in any ideals, programs, or norms. There is no goal so rational, no norm so right, no program so exemplary, no social ideal so attractive, no legitimacy or legality so compelling as to justify men's killing one another. . . . A war does not make sense by virtue of being fought for ideals or over rights, but by virtue of being fought against an actual foe.[10]

Obviously Schmitt is all too willing to go beyond mere tough-mindedness to outright bloody-mindedness. But before we impute this willingness exclusively to his undeniable fascist irrationalism, we must acknowledge that modern history offers no examples whatever in which the application of moral, ideological, or juridi-cal criteria to the conduct of international affairs has effectively curbed international tensions or moderated the ferocity of military conflict.

Contrasting the Two Views

Let us now consider some important contrasts between Easton's and Schmitt's views of the business of rule. First, Easton's view is inward, concerned above all with the internal concerns of the polity. Schmitt's is outward, focused on the polity's external con-cerns. Second, the ultimate aspect of the human condition for Easton is scarcity; for Schmitt it is danger. Third, Easton puts forward what might be called an economistic view of politics: political processes, as he understands them, are concerned with assigning to individuals things that they can enjoy in their private capacities. In Schmitt's view the single function of politics, to preserve the security and integrity of the collectivity, can be of significance to individuals only insofar as they share membership in the collectivity. Easton's politics are epitomized in the deliber-ations of a legislative assembly or the rulings of a judge: symbolic, discursive, civilian. In Schmitt's vision such aspects of politics are secondary to sheer, factual armed force as the ultimate foundation of the collectivity's ability to mount or counter a military threat.

Finally, these two views represent a twentieth-century echo of a long-standing European intellectual debate over the nature of politics.[11] Easton's view, which echoes Thomas More's in *Utopia*, responds to the distinctive political experience of post-Norman England. In a country protected by the sea from the direct and continuous threat of aggressive neighbors, political thought and praxis naturally turn inward, adopting as their standard the well-being of the commonwealth (the very expression "commonwealth" is significant) and the shaping of internal hierarchies of honor and advantage. Here, public controversy, the safeguarding of rights, and the framing and enforcing of laws appear as the very essence of political business. Schmitt, by contrast, restates a distinctly Continental conception, one first and most sharply articulated by Machiavelli in the sixteenth century as the operational code of the emergent sovereign states of Western and Central Europe. Here the prime fact of political experience is the continuous threat, potential or actual, that each country poses to its neighbor's boundaries and the ensuing continuous struggle for an equilibrium acceptable to all countries involved. Under these conditions political thought and praxis necessarily turn outward, according the highest priority to diplomacy and war.

Whatever the shortcomings of Easton's and Schmitt's views, I doubt that any other view of modern politics at this conceptual level deserves equal consideration. In particular, the Marxian view of politics, focused on the use of organized, society-wide coercion to secure (or end) the dominance of a class possessing the means of production, can probably be seen as a critical variant of Easton's view. Although the Marxian view, with its emphasis on coercion and class conflict, has a tough-mindedness missing from Easton's, the two views share a primary reference to allocative processes taking place within a collectivity understood in the first instance as a division of labor.

Reconciling the Two Views

The extreme contrast between Easton's and Schmitt's views makes all the more striking their agreement on one basic structural feature of political business, namely that whatever agency is responsible for that business must have privileged access to facilities for physical coercion. To be sure, Easton insists less than Schmitt that such access need be exclusive, and sees the exercise of coercion as typically occurring internally rather than externally. But their common emphasis on the necessity of coercion suggests that the two views may somehow be reconciled: indeed, that each may perhaps be seen as stating one aspect of politics rather than a self-sufficient, integral view of the whole.

It might seem reasonable at first to reconcile the two views by simply conceding Schmitt's and granting Easton's a kind of second-line validity. After all, the direct concern with preserving a collectivity's territorial and cultural integrity and historical continuity seemingly takes both logical and chronological precedence over the mere internal allocation of the values its members produce. It seems almost absurd, by contrast, to subordinate Schmitt's view to Easton's—to derive the very maintenance of the collectivity's independent existence from the business of internal value allocation.

But things are not that simple. Entirely apart from its repulsive moral undertones, Schmitt's view suffers from too many serious inadequacies to serve as an adequate point of departure. His chief error is to take the collectivity of reference (Us) as a datum, from which he goes on to stress how fragile, threatened, and conditional that datum is. But to *constitute* the collectivity, to impart to it the distinctiveness or sense of common destiny that politics, as Schmitt understands it, is designed to safeguard—all this, surely, is political business of the highest order. The collectivity is not a datum. It is itself the product of politics, which must first create it and can only then defend it. And in creating the collectivity in the first place, politics can hardly do without precisely those symbolic public processes that Easton emphasizes and Schmitt disdains.

Where Easton for his part errs is in seeing those processes as amounting to politics only insofar as they bear upon value allocations. As we have seen, values must be generated before they can be allocated; and the generating may well be more important than the allocating. Furthermore, some of the values so generated—e.g. a public park, the right to vote—cannot be allocated between individuals, but can only be possessed and enjoyed collectively.

If there is something brutal and demoniac about Schmitt's concept of the political, there is something petty and philistine about Easton's. Politics is surely more than a process of allocating valued objects carried out before greedy eyes by the grasping hands of a multitude of "antagonistic cooperators." Catlin is closer when he defines politics as "concerned with the relations of men, in association and competition, submission and control, in so far as they seek, not the production and consumption of some article, but to have their way with their fellow men."[12] Yet it is hard to see how else than through those processes Easton emphasizes—the framing and sanctioning of collectively binding decisions, the explicit patterning of interaction, the achievement and maintenance of internal order—collectivities can ever attain the distinctive identity that Schmitt sees as their essence.

Perhaps Schmitt is in some sense right in suggesting that collectivities can only define their identity by denying others what they regard as theirs. But how can a collectivity discriminate between friend and foe if not by referring to a conception of what makes Us into Us; and how can such a conception be generated except by ordering in some distinctive fashion the internal life of the collectivity? But if this is so, why deny the term "political" to the processes by which such a conception is produced and maintained against the threat of internal disorder?

In sum, if we divest Easton's inward-looking conception of its overemphasis on allocation and extend it to comprehend values central to the collectivity that can be possessed by its members only jointly and not singly, we have a view that points just as surely as

Schmitt's to a prime, distinctive, essential aspect of politics. The two views are in effect complementary. Much as one might discount Schmitt's view as demoniac or fascist,[13] history has repeatedly borne him out. Once the dangerousness and the ultimate disorderliness of social life are recognized, their implications remain utterly amoral and—today more than ever—utterly frightening. For all the advances of the last two centuries, we have as much reason today to hope with Adam Smith, and as little reason to believe, that "the inhabitants of all the different quarters of the world may arrive at that equality of courage and force which, by inspiring mutual fear, can alone overawe the injustice of independent nations into some sort of respect for the rights of one another."[14]

The Theory of Institutional Differentiation

So far we have sought to identify some basic requirements of social existence involving activities that can be meaningfully labeled "political." We have not asked how those requirements are attended to, how those activities are patterned, except to the extent of suggesting that rule always involves a more or less exclusive disposition over means of coercion. These are the questions that will occupy the rest of this book. In the light of the broad concept discussed in this chapter, our concern will be to examine the development over time of the distinctive structural features of one system of rule, the modern state.

Since it is in the very nature of the modern state that there should be many states, and since modern states have historically exhibited an enormous variety of institutional arrangements, clearly one speaks of *the* modern state as *one* system of rule only at a high level of abstraction. At such a level it seems appropriate to some sociologists to regard the formation of the modern state as an instance of "institutional differentiation," the process whereby the major functional problems of a society give rise in the course of time to various increasingly elaborated and distinctive sets of structural arrangements. In this view, the formation of the modern state parallels and complements various similar processes of institutional differentiation affecting, say, the economy, the family, and religion.

This approach has illustrious proponents both among the great sociologists of the past, who used it to get a conceptual hold on the nature of modern society, and among their contemporary epigones.[15] It also has attractive links to other disciplines dealing with evolutionary change. And it can be applied at various levels. Thus one might say that the key phenomenon in the development of the modern state was the institutionalization, within "modernizing" Western societies, of the distinction between the private/social realm and the public/political realm, and that the same process was later carried further within each realm. In the public realm, for instance, the "division of powers" assigned different functions of rule to different constitutional organs; in the private realm, the occupational system became further differentiated from, say, the sphere of the family. And so on.

Thus a proponent of this approach has the considerable advantage of applying a single more or less elaborate model of the differentiation process, with appropriate specifications and adjustments, to a great range of events, showing how in each case the same "logic" operates. And indeed at several points in this book I have found this approach useful. But on the whole I have not adopted it, for three reasons.

First, by its affinity (often explicitly asserted) with biological evolutionism, the approach seems to claim the status of a proper scientific theory, notably the ability to explain the phenomena it discusses. Yet entirely apart from the question of whether sociologists may legitimately aspire to such an aim, no one has yet specified mechanisms of social evolution with anywhere near the explanatory power of those worked out for natural evolution by Darwin or Mendel.[16]

Second, whatever its strengths or weaknesses, the theory postulates a cumulative, irreversible process of differentiation. Thus it can shed no light, explanatory or otherwise, on those recent phenomena that are tending to displace the distinction between state and society, thus suggesting a process not of differentiation but of de-differentiation.

Finally, any attempt to render the institutional story of the modern state purely in terms of a general theory of social change can at best trace the diffusion of the state as an existing entity from its European heartland to outlying areas. But that is not enough for our purposes in this book. Such a general theory cannot encompass the state's origins. It cannot identify within a given society the distinctive forces and interests ("material and ideal," in Weber's terms) from whose interaction that new system of rule emerged. Nor can it begin to do justice to such weighty components of the development of the modern state as the Greek conception of the political process, with its distinctive duality of public argument at one end and enforceable law at the other;[17] the religious individualism and universalism of Christianity;[18] and the Germanic view that encroachment upon one's rights can be legitimately resisted even against one's own superior.[19]

I cannot claim that the typological treatment attempted in the following chapters gives such factors their full due. I hope only that by employing a scheme in which they have a place, I can take the reader beyond the relatively shallow notion of "institutional differentiation" to a deeper insight into the complexity of the historical events that have gone into the making of the modern state.

CHAPTER II

The Feudal System of Rule

THIS CHAPTER and the two that follow discuss a historical sequence of three types of rule systems: feudalism, the *Ständestaat*, and absolutism. This typology has often been used by students of the historical and legal aspects of political institutions working within the German tradition; students from the French and the Anglo-American traditions have been less familiar with it, or have shown themselves less inclined to concede the structural distinctiveness of the Ständestaat (a term to be explained below) as an intermediate system between feudalism, on the one hand, and absolutism, on the other.[1] A further objection to this typology will undoubtedly be raised by those many historians who balk at reducing the vastness and diversity of human events and arrangements (for rule, in this case) to a few sharply contrasted conceptual devices. Yet such a practice is unavoidable in a work of sociology aimed at making comparative statements or some kind of developmental synthesis, and I follow some notable precedents in treating about one thousand years in the history of Western political institutions through a sequence of only three constructs, each more closely approximating the "mature modern state" of the nineteenth century.[2]

My starting point is the creation of the Carolingian empire, which I take as the context of the rise of the feudal system of rule. The switch to the Ständestaat system I place, in most of the lands under consideration, between the late twelfth and early fourteenth centuries; that from the Ständestaat to the absolutist system of rule I place between the sixteenth and seventeenth centuries. By the early eighteenth century, absolutism was already on the decline in some important countries under the pressure of developments—many of them not of a specifically political nature—that I shall designate as "the rise of civil society." (The expression *ancien régime*, at any rate in the narrow meaning it has in Tocqueville,[3] can be seen as another designation for this last transition.)

The geographical focus of the discussion is on continental Western Europe, especially the lands now making up Germany and France. I include developments in the Iberian peninsula, too, but generally leave to one side those in the Italian peninsula. The "English case," particularly after feudalism, does not fit easily into the argument, even in the highly abstract terms in which I phrase it. To a lesser extent, the same thing can be said of Scandinavia. On the other hand, parts of Eastern Europe—particularly Prussia, the Baltic lands, and those areas progressively brought under Hapsburg domination—may be seen as "covered" by the argument for some periods and aspects of their political history. However, I pay little attention to the regional and national variants of the rule systems in question, and refer to developments in individual countries only for general examples.[4]

The Rise of Feudalism

Although the typology introduced at the beginning of this chapter concerns the development of Western *political* institutions, each system of rule must be seen against a broader background of cultural, economic, social, and technological phenomena. All these phenomena were continually changing during the period under examination here (late eighth to early fourteenth centuries), but we may begin by considering the features characteristic of the early part of the period and relating them to the establishment of feudalism as a system of rule.[5] Before the outset of our period, three developments had profoundly disrupted the material and institutional landscape of Western Europe: (1) the breakdown of the Western Roman Empire, both as a centralized system of government and as an administrative system centered around municipalities; (2) the massive dislocation of populations in the *Völkerwanderungen*; and (3) the shift away from the Mediterranean of the main lines of communication and trade among Western European populations and between them and others.

From these developments stemmed some features of the historical context whose significance for the establishment and management of a system of rule is fairly apparent: widespread disruption, disrepair, and insecurity of the lines of transport and communication; thoroughgoing decommercialization of economic processes, now almost exclusively isolated rural undertakings operating at very low levels of productivity and unable to rely on support and demand from the urban centers, themselves mostly in a state of abandon and economically weak; an extremely low level of literacy, with reading and writing practically a monopoly of the clergy and confined to Latin, which outside the clergy is ceasing to be a *lingua franca*; and a population attaining at best very low levels of nutrition, health, comfort, and security, with the result that life expectancy is appallingly short and population density in many areas below viable levels.

All things considered, it is not unreasonable to apply the designation "Dark Ages," however biased in tone, to this historical context. Yet within it, in the latter part of the eighth century, the Carolingian dynasty ambitiously (and for a few decades successfully) undertook to reconstitute a comprehensive, translocal framework of rule. It sought thereby to recover the now distant and dimly perceived Roman legacy of order and unity, and to impart to the social existence of Western Christianity a greater measure of coherence, of security from invasion, banditry, naked oppression, and misery, than the ecclesiastical system of leadership alone could provide.

The celebrated event that marks the culmination of this undertaking—the crowning of Charlemagne, king of the Franks since

768, emperor in Rome by the Pope on Christmas Day, 800[6]—visibly reveals two major components of the undertaking: the reference to Imperial Rome, and the close association with Christianity and the Church. To these correspond two significant aspects of the system of rule the Carolingians sought to operate. First, there was the attempt to structure rule vertically through the establishment of two distinctively public offices; I refer here to the appointment of *comites* (counts) and *missi dominici* (envoys of the ruler), the latter having the responsibility for activating and controlling at intervals, according to central directives, the business of rule carried out locally by the former. Second, there was the reliance on bishoprics and abbeys (whose boundaries often corresponded to those of the Roman municipalities and large landed estates, respectively) as the main horizontal elements of the administrative structure.

But a third component of the original Carolingian design was not as visibly in evidence as the Roman and the ecclesiastical ones in the ceremony of Christmas Day, 800. Yet this element, of barbaric and particularly of Germanic origin, was to make a profound, and in the long run largely destructive, impact upon the new system of rule. This was the relationship of *Gefolgschaft*, "followership," a personal bond of mutual loyalty and affection between a warrior chief and his hand-picked retinue of close associates, his trusted companions in honor, adventure, and leadership.[7] Already widespread in 800, these typically close and highly personal relationships between near-peers were to become an indispensable institutional component of the Carolingian empire, and were to survive its demise and deeply affect Western arrangements for rule for several centuries afterward.

Why was this so? Let us reconsider the historical context sketched out above—in particular, the insecurity and irregularity of communications; the impossibility, under conditions approximating the notion of a "natural" (as against a "money") economy, of building up through taxes a treasury from which to finance an apparatus of rule actually run from the center; and the necessity, in the face of invasion and banditry, of orienting the business of rule primarily to *military* tasks. Clearly, under such conditions it was impossible to maintain a unitary political system based exclusively on counts and *missi dominici*, and in which the latter were to be treated as holders of public, centrally bestowed and controlled faculties of rule, supported from public funds, and subject to territorial rotation, recall, accountability, and dismissal. Such offices (and up to a point, too, the ecclesiastical ones) had to be qualified and complemented by understandings and arrangements derived essentially from Gefolgschaft, from the notion of the chosen retinue of warriors clustered around the chief.

The Nature of the Feudal Relationship

To become a vital component of the feudal system of rule, Gefolgschaft itself had to be enriched and qualified by institutional traits not themselves of Germanic or barbaric origin, but rather of late Roman origin. These traits are best signaled by the Latin designations of three significant arrangements.

Commendatio. This was originally a highly skewed relationship whereby an inferior (though normally free) party entrusted himself to the protection of a superior, powerful one, and assumed toward him duties of submission (if not outright subjection) and, when necessary, of personal aid.

Beneficium (later *fevum*, then *feudum*; hence "fief"). This was a grant of rights, chiefly to land but including the land's population (slave, serf, or free) and agricultural appurtenances, intended to supply the material needs of an individual or community taking charge of some ecclesiastical or governmental responsibility.

Immunitas. Here, the household and possessions of an individual or a collectivity (the latter generally ecclesiastical) became exempt from the fiscal, military, and judicial powers normally exercised by the holder of a public office over the territory including them.

In the feudal system of rule, these three arrangements became integrated with Gefolgschaft, modifying it and being modified by it. The result was a profound (and for a long time irreversible) dislocation of the vertical axis of the original Carolingian design—the relationship between the emperor, at one end, and the counts and *missi*, at the other. Let us see how this happened.

As a result of the influence of Gefolgschaft, the prefeudal commendatio lost some of its skewness, as it were; its gradient became less steep. Both in its typical content and in the ritual forms of its enactment, the commendatio gradually came to be perceived as a suitable arrangement for two parties who were in principle near-peers (as in the Gefolgschaft). This is not to say that the new, feudal commendatio assumed total equality between the parties, or made their respective obligations totally symmetrical or otherwise equivalent. Nonetheless, there was enough equality to indicate that the party who "commended" himself (the vassal) and the party who received the commendatio (the lord) belonged in principle to the same, exclusive social world. Typically, both were practitioners of the same mode of warfare, one that required great skill and that was economically and physically exacting: shock combat between mounted, heavily armored warriors. The relation between the parties to the commendatio committed the lord to protect the vassal, the vassal to lend his aid and advice to the lord, and both to hold each other in affection and respect. They thus acknowledged each other as companions, just as the members of the Germanic Gefolgschaft were expected to do toward one another and toward the chief they jointly followed. Thus understood, the feudal commendatio is something more than a relationship at once contractual (i.e., resting on the free, reciprocal choice of the partners and generating mutual obligations) and hierarchical (i.e., recognizing some degree of inequality between the parties); it is also, in its typical form, colored by emotional content (loyalty, affection, trust, comradeship) not often found in either contractual or hierarchical relations. It is thus an intensely *personal* relation, envisaging two partners who choose, aid, and respect each other as individuals.

The beneficium (fief) was affected by the notion of Gefolgschaft by being drawn into the arrangements of the feudal commendatio. A fief was granted by the lord to the vassal on the under-

21

standing that by exploiting it economically the vassal would be enabled to render the services he owed the lord: to equip himself with weapons and mounts; to train, equip, reward, and lead an esquire and the small team of subalterns necessary to support a mounted warrior in the field; to join the lord's host or his council when required; to maintain a household befitting one who was a near-peer of the lord, and often his guest or host; and so forth. Thus the land grant was implicitly, and often explicitly, a corollary to the logic of the commendatio: indeed, it came to constitute a much more significant expression of the lord's favor than the simple promise of protection and amity to the vassal. In fact, the grant of the fief was designed precisely to enable the vassal to look after his *own* protection and that of his dependents, and if necessary to aid the lord.

As for immunitas, originally its significance was chiefly negative: an "immune" household and estate simply constituted a gap within the territorial reach of the powers normally exercised by the grantor, an enclave where his writ did not run. Feudalism attached positive significance to the same phenomenon. Insofar as it became tied to the commendatio and the grant of land, immunity entailed that the vassal was not just permitted but expected to exercise over his fief a number of prerogatives of rule—levying contributions (in kind, in labor, possibly in specie), declaring and enforcing the law, defending and policing the land, leading armed dependents into battle, and so on. The vassal was expected to do all this on his own behalf, using his prerogatives as a means to the economic exploitation of the land he held in grant and of its resident dependents. His doing so was itself construed as a vital aspect of his service to the lord; it was a means of decentralizing, of extending into the periphery, the lord's own activities of rule.

Thus, to repeat, the fief became built into the commendatio; the lord's obligation to leave the vassal undisturbed ("immune") in the possession and governance of the fief became the most significant counterpart to the vassal's obligation to aid and counsel his lord, and to extend and mediate his powers at the local level. At the same time, the fief constituted the source of the vassal's economic self-sufficiency and the spatial frame of the exercise of his rights (and duties) of command.

In this way, on the one hand the relationship built around the fief bound into a complex elaboration of the original Gefolgschaft two individuals who belonged, by birth or by proven vocation, to the same high social stratum of leaders and warriors (and who were also rentiers, since their military preoccupations and social standing were not compatible with their taking too active a part in the management of their possessions). On the other hand, the relationship voluntarily entered into by the two near-peers had significant effects on vast numbers of humbler people (peasants, villeins, domestic dependents, serfs, and sometimes slaves), who simply had to submit to those effects. Such people, of course, made up the great majority of the population, except in the few regions where the peasantry were mostly settled on *allodia*, i.e., lands not subject to feudal burdens. For the great bulk of the population, then, the "skew" in rule relationships that feudal developments had "flattened" between the parties in the commendatio sharply increased. Such people were deeply affected by the feudal relationship without being parties to it; the parties themselves looked on them essentially as the objects of rule, and occasionally and incidentally as the beneficiaries of rule, but never as the subjects of a political relationship. The economic aspects of the feudal relationship, too, were essentially oriented to the advantage of the vassal as rentier and consumer.

The lord-vassal relation—the cell, as it were, of the feudal system of rule—should thus be viewed as lying right at the edge of a steep gradient dividing both its partners from the lower social groups. The steepness of that gradient stemmed from the sharp inequalities in the relationship between the vassal and his dependents and social inferiors, a relationship denoted by the term *seigneurie*.[8] The vassal's rights inherent in seigneurie, to lead, control, exploit, and often oppress his dependents, presupposed (and reinforced) an inequality between the parties long absent from the commendatio. Seigneurial relations were not wholly devoid of reciprocities, some of which were the same in content and emotional undertones as those in feudal relations (particularly the exchange of protection for loyalty). But seigneurial relations were of a different institutional nature from lord-vassal ones; after all, they often connected a warrior with serfs of a different ethnic and linguistic group.

The abuses to which seigneurial relations often led were bitterly commented on by Estienne de Fougères, himself a member of the knightly estate: "The knight ought to take the sword in order to render justice and fend off those who cause ills to others. But the majority escape these obligations. . . . They collect the rents due them, . . . then go on bothering and deceiving [the people], giving no thought to the protection they owe them. . . . And yet we ought to cherish our men, since the villeins bear the burdens on which depends the livelihood of all of us—knights, clerics, and masters."[9]

If we conceive of the feudal relation as entailing significant effects (for good or ill) for those who were not parties to it, then we can see that it would function as the chief structural component of a wider, comprehensive system of rule, extending over larger populations, by being replicated and extended *upward*: the knight who protected and exploited the villeins did so as the vassal of a lord who might in turn have been the vassal of a higher lord still. In two or three steps this extension and replication of the feudal relationship would arrive at an overlord bearing typically a title of Roman origin (*rex*, *princeps*, *dux*); this overlord claims a greater plenitude of faculties of rule than those normally allocated through the feudal relation proper, and seeks to exercise them with reference to a *territory* rather than to individual sections of land held in feudal tenure. (In the rest of this chapter and in the following two I shall refer to an overlord of this kind as the "territorial ruler.")

Historically, however, the elaboration of the lord-vassal relation mostly advanced *downward*. Typically, a territorial ruler, finding it impossible to operate a system of rule constituted of impersonal, official roles, sought to bridge the gap between himself and the ultimate objects of rule—the populace—by relying primarily on his retinue of trusted warriors. To this end, he endowed them with fiefs from the landed domain under his charge (which he treated as the patrimony of his dynasty); but his immediate vassals often carved from their own fiefs smaller ones for the members of *their* retinues.

At other times, the territorial ruler might use the feudal relation to strengthen his ties to the holders of offices (as with the counts and, below them, the counts' deputies or *vicarii*). But his successors might then find that the feudal component in the position of such individuals (and *their* successors) had become preponderant over the official component, with its obligations of impersonal service and accountability; in other words, the fief, with its lucrative seigneurial rights, was now much the more salient feature of their relations to the lord than the office. On yet other occasions, wealthy and powerful lords might force their nominal overlord to enter into somewhat constrained feudal relations with themselves as vassals simply to make their own possessions more secure.[10]

Trends in the System

Under different circumstances, and with different tempos in different lands, between the middle of the ninth and the middle of the eleventh century the feudal relation became the key component of the system of rule in most of the territories covered by my argument. In most places it left its imprint on the ecclesiastical system of offices, too; in many, it sharply proclaimed its exclusiveness in the maxim *nulle terre sans seigneur*—a maxim significant not only with respect to the phenomenon of rule as such, but also with respect to the overlapping framework of property relations and the mode of production.

The relevance of this development to my argument is that it made a network of interpersonal relations into the chief carrying structure of rule. To use Theodor Mayer's somewhat anachronistic phrase, it amounted to building up "the state as an association of persons."[11]* But the "state" so constituted possessed an inherent tendency to shift the seat of effective power, the fulcrum of rule, downward toward the lower links in the chain of lord-vassal relations. To this extent the "feudal state" is one that undermines itself, making unified rule over large areas increasingly difficult.

Georges Duby's outstanding monograph on the Mâconnais—an area in what is today east-central France—supplies an example of this long-term phenomenon.[12] In this area where the king of France was a dimly perceived, politically ineffective figure, the main change in the system of rule during the eleventh and twelfth centuries was the weakening of the count's position and the shift of his powers to pettier lords, particularly those who had erected or come into possession of castles (the *castellani*, or castellans). By the late eleventh century, the count's *plaid* (court) had become a pseudojudicial, patrimonial organ of exclusively private significance. The castellans no longer attended it, for they had already incorporated the powers over the rural population originally *delegated* to them by the count into their patrimonies. Thus the count could no longer exercise direct leadership over the free men of his territory.

Each castle in the county had become "a center of rule independent of the [count's] main castle; the seat of a court settling disputes independently of the count's court; the rallying place of a clientele of vassals competing with that centered on the count." Each powerful castellan exploited to his own advantage prerogatives of rule over the outlying peasants, from military levies and exactions to criminal and civil jurisdiction. As a result:

The nature itself of rule has become transformed. One no longer distinguishes between the power of *ban*, which, owing to its origin in the king's might, was previously considered a higher form of command, and the *de facto* domination individuals enjoy over their own private

* Note references followed by asterisks indicate notes that contain substantive material in addition to citations.

dependents. . . . All those who protect and lead are considered to be on the same plane. The hierarchy of powers has been replaced by a criss-crossing pattern of competing networks of clients. General and sharply defined duties toward the community as a whole have been replaced by individual arrangements for limited and different services: the commitment of the vassal to his lord, the submission of the humble dependent to his *dominus*.[13]

As Duby and many others have shown, the main trend through most (but not all) of the feudal period was the fragmenting of each large system of rule into many smaller, and increasingly autonomous, systems that differed widely in the way they carried out the business of rule and that were often at war with one another. Let us see what lies behind this trend.

First, from early on it was normal for each lord to have more than one vassal. Since in principle each feudal relationship was entered *intuitu personae*, that is by taking into account the individuality of the participants, the mutual obligations of lord and vassal could differ considerably from relationship to relationship. As a result, the lord's relationship to the ultimate objects of rule, the populace, was mediated differently by each vassal. The size of the fief, the exact terms on which it was granted, the rights of rule over it that remained with the lord or that were vested in the vassal—as these aspects of the basic relationship varied, so did the modalities and content of the exercise of rule. Its day-to-day routines might thus differ considerably even between adjacent fiefs carved out of the same lord's landholdings. The differences in the terms on which a lord enfeoffed his several vassals might be further compounded by the diverse terms under which the former, as a vassal himself, held land from a higher lord.

Second, one man could become the vassal of more than one lord, which further increased the diversity in the ways fiefs were held, exploited, and ruled. Furthermore, should one vassal's several lords quarrel with one another and all appeal to that vassal's aid and support, the latter might use this confused situation as a pretext for suspending his obligations toward all of them and asserting his independence. The complexity such arrangements were capable of generating in the pattern of feudal relations can be glimpsed in the statement given by Robert, count of Gloucester, at an inquest held in 1133 on behalf of Henry I of England, "into the fiefs held by barons, knights, and *vavassores* of the Church of the Blessed Mary of Bayeux" in Normandy:

> I am one of the barons of the Blessed Mary, my lady, and I inherited the right to be her standard-bearer, and I hold the fiefs of ten knights from Evreux. I owe the service of one knight to the benefit of the king of France. For the benefit of the lord of Normandy I owe the service of two knights in the marches for forty days, always from the same fief. Furthermore, for the fief of Roger Suhart, which is a fief of eight knights, and for the fief of Malfiliâtre, which is a fief for seven knights I hold from the bishop of Bayeux, I owe for the service of the king of France a knight and a half, and for service in the marches of Normandy three knights for forty days. And when the duke summons the host, I owe him through the bishop all the knights whose fiefs I hold from the bishop.[14]

Third, if a vassal in turn granted parts of his fief to one or more lower vassals, he did not create a *direct* relationship between his own lord and these lower vassals.[15]* Thus what we might call the top-to-bottom coherence of the system was low: the chances were poor that a given lord's undertakings would be supported unanimously and in a coordinated fashion by all those vassals who ultimately "held of him" at various removes. Postinvasion England was a significant exception from this standpoint, for there the king by and large made good his claim to be considered and obeyed (on specified matters) as the overlord of *all* lords and vassals in the land, no matter how many links away in the chain of subinfeudations. But on the Continent, despite the existence of the obscure and disputed notion of suzerainty, by which, from the eleventh century on, certain lords held that they could make some claims on their own vassals' vassals, the fragmentation of authority continued.

These three factors weakening the effective control of the higher feudal powers over the pettier ones were compounded by three momentous developments in the lord-vassal bond. First, that bond's duration ceased to be contingent upon certain performances on the vassal's part. The circumstances under which the vassal had to hand over the fief to his lord became reduced to outright treachery and blatant dereliction of duty—and even then the vassal might successfully resist the takeover by force. Second, where the maxim *nulle terre sans seigneur* obtained, it often imposed on the lord a "compulsion to grant" a fief returned to him for whatever reason; in other words, he *had* to grant it to another vassal and could not keep it among his own holdings.[16] Finally (and most significantly), the fief came to be considered part of the patrimony of the vassal's lineage—and thus divisible, inheritable, and sometimes alienable.

Two of these developments (the restriction of the "conditionality" of the feudal title and its inheritability) were expressly sanctioned by the Emperor Conrad II in 1037, while he was besieging Milan, with reference to his own Italian vassals:

> To reconcile the spirits of lords and vassals, and to the end that the latter should faithfully serve ourselves and their lords with constancy and devotion, we decree and firmly establish that no vassal who holds a fief—whether from bishops, abbots, abbesses, marquises, counts, or anybody else—from our public possessions or from those of churches, and who has been unjustly deprived of one, should lose his fief without a certain and demonstrated offense, on the basis of the statutes of our ancestors and of the judgment of the peers.
>
> We also decree that when a vassal, great or small, dies, his fief should go to his son.[17]

In this way, those faculties of rule that when exercised over the dependent rural populations constituted the most significant day-to-day expression of the feudal system of rule, and that from the beginning had been closely tied in with the business of extracting from subordinates labor, produce, rents, and tolls to their master's benefit, became increasingly just so many aspects of proprietary rights over the land.

Of course, in the period under discussion landed property was something very different when held under feudal title than when held otherwise (as *allodium*, i.e., unencumbered with feudal charges), and was even more different from what it was to become with the commercialization of the countryside in the modern era. As we have seen, feudal lands were crisscrossed by plural, overlapping jurisdictions generated by "jumbled" lord-vassal relations; moreover, villages and churches often laid claim by tradition to the use of land and its produce. Nonetheless, the developments in the feudal relationship discussed above had generally fused the jurisdictional-political and the proprietary-economic prerogatives of fiefholders in such a way that the purely patrimonial component became progressively dominant, until the landed estate itself came to be seen as the inherent carrier of semipolitical, formerly public prerogatives conferred upon its holder by virtue simply of the fact of his holding it—with at most a ritual reference to a granting lord and to the original terms and intents of the grant.[18]

The development of progressively greater autonomy on the part of fiefholders generated increasing numbers of jurisdictional rivalries and boundary disputes, which were difficult to settle by appeals to the increasingly nominal rights of higher lords and suzerains. Under these conditions, parties confronted with what they saw as violations of their rights considered it legitimate to undertake themselves the forcible redress of those violations in forms varying from tightly regulated judicial duels (between the principals or their champions) to savage, prolonged "private wars."[19] This followed from the very nature of the feudal relation, which originally tied together two professional warriors, each bound by a code of honor to stand up—and fight, if necessary—for his rights even against the other. Furthermore, since each lord or vassal was expected to provide his own means of keeping order among his dependents and defending them from outsiders, it was only natural to find those means turned from time to time against other lords or vassals. In fact, as I have indicated, it was expected that coercion would be employed (or, more often, threatened) to extract surplus from one's serfs and peasants; its employment against somebody else's serfs and peasants was but an extension (and a frequent one) of that notion.

These are the institutional roots of what is often referred to as "feudal anarchy." It arose from the fact that the system of rule relied, both for order-keeping and for the enforcement of rights and the redress of wrongs, on self-activated coercion exercised by a small, privileged class of warriors and rentiers in their own interest. The extremities of oppression and violence that such an approach to law and order generated can be inferred from the text of an oath the bishops of Beauvais and Soissons, acting on behalf of the faithful in their respective dioceses, asked the feudatories of the Reims area to take in 1023:

I shall not break forcibly into any church, nor into the stores of any church, except with the intent of apprehending a wretched violator of the peace or an assassin. I shall not imprison any peasants or their wives, nor any merchants; I shall not seize their money or compel them to free themselves by paying a ransom. I do not intend for them to lose their possessions on account of some local war fought by their lord, nor will I have them flogged in order to seize their means of sustenance. I will neither destroy nor burn down their houses. I will not pull up the roots of their vineyards, not even by claiming that it is necessary for the conduct of war; nor will I use that same pretext to seize their wine.[20]

The Political Legacy of the Feudal System

For the many reasons set forth above, the design of employing the feudal relationship as the key component in a structure of rule complementary to that based on public (and ecclesiastical) offices was historically unsuccessful.[21] The growth of feudalism led, in most parts of Western Europe, to a drastic erosion of the landed patrimony of territorial rulers, who granted fiefs in order to tie to themselves men who in turn replicated the process downward toward pettier vassals. Feudal features so overlaid the official structure, which was centered on the territorial rulers and their households, that that structure lost its distinctiveness and its effectiveness. As we have seen, the center of political gravity shifted toward ever narrower and more locally rooted centers of rule, which grew increasingly independent of one another. Hence there developed acute problems of coordination, crises of order, and recurrent and apparently anarchic violence.

Furthermore, as I have indicated, the feudal relationship itself underwent a change in its internal structure that caused it to lose even the virtues of its own defects: the growth of heritability and other developments mentioned above weakened the appeal to the mutual loyalty of two near-peers, linked by a commendatio, that had at first been seen as a reliable, emotionally potent, culturally creditable bond between a ruler and his personal associates in rule. The feudal relationship, one might say, became depersonalized, but not by institutionalizing more general, abstract, rationally ordered understandings and patterns of rule; rather, the relationship became bound up with a lineage's exclusive particularism, its dynastic pride, its fierce commitment to maintaining and increasing its patrimony, to asserting its status.[22]*

For all this, feudalism as a system of rule does not represent entirely the "year naught" in the story of the modern state.[23] It constituted a first attempt to impose a firm and workable framework of rule on lands that had suffered much devastation and insecurity; and though it could not withstand its own internal entropy, it never entirely negated the original design, never utterly obliterated the distinctiveness and superiority of the old imperial, kingly, and princely titles, offices, and prerogatives, however remote they may have become in terms of day-to-day rule.

Also, feudalism rooted in the land (to exploit, but at the same time to govern and protect, its population) a warrior class that had often come from afar and had strong nomadic tendencies. To this class feudalism attributed powers that went beyond those of a purely military nature, and in the exercise of which these warriors slowly but progressively learned to consider criteria of equity, to respect local traditions, to protect the weak, and to practice responsibility. The European nobility that slowly emerged from the feudalization of the original warrior class became the primordial estate of the future Ständestaat—an estate of men trained in leadership and in initiating collective action, and one destined by its highly privileged position to promote pursuits and standards of aesthetic accomplishment and civilized existence to which European culture at large owes a great debt.[24]

Furthermore, even prior to and independently of the rediscovery of Roman law and the sophisticated elaboration of canon law, feudalism established the notion that argument (however irrationally and violently conducted) about rights and justice (however particularistically understood) constituted the standard way of setting the boundaries of rule and of confronting and correcting misrule: moreover, it forced the appeal to armed might to justify itself in those terms.[25]

Albeit as members of a narrow, exclusive, exploitative minority, individuals acquired claims that they could lawfully uphold with their own strength against one another and *even against their superiors*.[26] In a letter of 1022 to Robert of France, for instance, Eudes, count of Blois, explains that he has decided not to attend a court session arranged to judge him by the king because he has learned of the king's determination not to accept any judgment that would make Eudes worthy of holding benefices from him in the future. (In the extract that follows, the term "honor" probably means both a charge of public origin with attendant possessions *and* honor in our sense of the term.)

I very much wonder that you, O lord, should have judged me unworthy of your benefices so precipitately, without discussing the cause. In fact, if the condition of my kin is considered, anybody would grant that I am worthy of inheriting. As to the benefice I held of you, it is apparent that it is part not of your kingly possessions but of those that thanks to your favor I received by inheritance from my ancestors. And if the significance of my service is in question, you well know how I have served you in peace, in war, and on your travels, as long as you held me in your favor. But once you withdrew that favor from me and sought to deprive me of the honor you had given me, if I did anything that you found offensive while defending myself and my honor, I was pushed into it by the wrong done me and under the pressure of necessity. Indeed, how could I fail to defend my honor? I call to witness God and my own soul that I would rather die with honor than to live deprived of it. But if you do not insist upon taking away my honor,

I desire nothing in the world more than having and deserving your favor.[27]

One might argue that in thus establishing the right of some individuals to resist a prevaricating ruler, feudalism created (or perhaps received from a Germanic inheritance and handed on) a distinctively Western legal conception destined to a long and glorious future.

Finally, it should be noted that in the above sketch I have somewhat overemphasized the downward shift of the center of political gravity by considering mainly the trends in the development of the feudal system of rule in its early and middle phases—from the Carolingian empire, say, to the middle or late eleventh century. In a later phase, those trends were slowly and haltingly resisted and even inverted, ultimately to the advantage of the territorial rulers (particularly but not exclusively in France). As we have seen, these rulers bore titles of Roman origin; their charge was often surrounded by a distinctive, sacred aura imparted to them by ritual (see the Germanic *Königsweihe* or the French *sacre du roi*) not itself originally of a feudal nature; they were often assisted by a small body of close advisers and helpers (relatives, clergymen, high household dependents) that again was not held together by feudal ties. Yet interestingly, these rulers, in justifying their drives against "feudal anarchy" and "baronial insubordination," often employed the feudal language of rights, and particularly the notion of suzerainty (which thus became confusingly associated with the emerging notion of sovereignty).[28]

Duby, again, clearly documents this phenomenon from the second half of the twelfth century, when the king of France rose again from behind the horizon of effective rule in the Mâconnais. At first the wars he conducted to curb the independence of this or that local lord were "private wars"; the alliances he formed to divide and rule were feudal agreements between near-peers; the recognition and support he claimed from the various *potentes* were those due the suzerain.[29] Generally, territorial rulers used feudal language (though they modified it) in seeking to establish within the feudatory class a relatively coherent hierarchy coextensive with their territories. In particular, they elaborated and enriched what was originally a feudal vocabulary to devise a widely understood "pecking order" of noble titles, each of which slowly became associated with specific packages of privileges, prerogatives, claims to honor and precedence, and attendant responsibilities.

The use of feudal devices in the context of what appears in retrospect to have been a distinctively "transfeudal"[30] historical undertaking—the building of modern states by and around territorial rulers—should not be considered as indicating intentional duplicity on the part of those rulers. Many of their dynasties had held for generations a thoroughly feudal definition of their own prerogatives; and just as vassals had come to consider their fiefs part of their patrimonies, so the princely dynasties had learned to conceive of the territories they ruled as their own patrimonies.

An obsession with territorial aggrandizement through marriages, inheritances, partitions, barters, reversions of fiefs, and acquisitions of land was to remain characteristic of those dynasties for many centuries to come.[31] But this did not prevent them from putting forward just as insistently their claims to a monopoly of distinctively "regalian" rights—high justice, the minting of coins, the designation of bishops and abbots, the concession of charters to towns, or the regulation of the latter's increasingly significant economic activities. But within the framework of my argument, this last phenomenon points beyond feudalism to the next term in our typology of systems of rule.

CHAPTER III

The Ständestaat

T HE SOCIOECONOMIC context against which, in the last chapter, I set the rise of the feudal system of rule in the eighth century had undergone numerous and profound changes by the thirteenth. Among those changes I shall emphasize, because of its significance both within and outside the political framework, the development of the towns. As I mentioned at the outset of the last chapter, I follow German practice in labeling the system of rule that was widespread by the thirteenth century in the lands under consideration here the Ständestaat, which might be rendered in English as "the polity of the Estates." Though the growth of the Ständestaat was not everywhere distinctly associated with the development of the towns—it was in Spain, for example, but was not in Hungary—generally speaking the emergence (or resurgence) of the towns throws considerable light on the "type switch" from feudalism to the Ständestaat.[1]

The Rise of Towns

To see why this was so, let us consider some political aspects of the rise of the towns at the beginning of the second millennium A.D. In the medieval West, towns developed not just as ecologically distinctive settings, as dense settlements of people attending to specifically urban productive and commercial pursuits, but also as politically autonomous entities.[2] Their autonomy was often gained against the expressed opposition and visible resistance either of the territorial ruler and his representatives (frequently bishops in Italy and Germany), or of the feudal element, or of both.

Thus the ascent of the towns marked the entrance of a new political force into a system of rule thus far dominated, at whatever level, by the two partners in the lord-vassal relation. At the very least, such a force had to be taken into account in the shifting equilibrium between the territorial ruler and his feudatories, if only as a possible ally to be used by one against the other. But there was more to it than this, for the towns typically asserted themselves—or reasserted themselves, after centuries of decay and abandon—in a way that was novel, if not utterly unprecedented, in that it involved the creation or political reactivation of *centers of solidary action by singly powerless individuals*. The towns thus claimed rights that were corporate in nature, i.e., that attached to individuals only by virtue of their membership in a constituted collectivity capable of operating as a unitary entity. There was an element of continuity here with the basic institutional inspiration of the feudal system, insofar as prerogatives of rule were being claimed and appropriated as a matter of "immunity," as "franchises" (often formally acknowledged in charters issued by the territorial ruler and framed in feudal language). But because these franchises were held collectively, they sanctioned, or helped the formation of, relatively wide commonalities.

Jan Dhondt has distinguished three patterns in the relationship between the franchise as an acknowledged (though often previously usurped) set of faculties of rule and the commonalities tying together the franchise-holders.

The first concerns Italy, where the formation of a collective consciousness precedes chronologically the concession of the franchises. The second concerns the "new towns," which are founded and chartered with the express intent of attracting a population by promising it certain privileges. Here the privilege itself serves largely as the basis for the development of collective consciousness, since the concession to the town dwellers of a distinctive legal *status* marked them off from the outlying rural environment. In the third pattern (probably the most frequent . . .), the inhabitants evolved a collective consciousness on the basis of shared interests. That consciousness was presupposed by the concession of franchises, though it could be strengthened by it. It was probably on the basis of common interests, and independently of privileges, that the townsmen linked up with one another in those "amical leagues" (*amitiés*) we read so much about in the sources.[3]

I should like to stress the conceptual novelty of this development, in all its variants, when viewed against the background of the feudal system of rule. We have seen that the feudal relation typically connected two parties who were both *potentes* to begin with, and that the vassal was given the fief not to make him powerful, but to allow him to preserve and exercise his previously acquired power. Furthermore, the lord-vassal relation was hierarchical, however moderated its "skew" may have been by the presumption that the parties were near-peers. Finally, once their bond had been sealed through the ritual homage and the fief granted, the two parties to the feudal relation expected to perform, and to an even greater extent did perform, their respective obligations separately; each stood secure in his own power, which he might occasionally be called upon to exercise in the other's behalf.

By contrast, the towns acquired power and political autonomy as aggregates formed and kept continuously in operation by the voluntary coalescence of the wills—and pooling of the resources—of individually powerless equals.[4] Once again a barbaric institution often inspired the original agreement and regulated its execution: this was not Gefolgschaft, "followership," as in the case of feudalism, but *Genossenschaft*, "companionship," "fellowship." In the Romance-language areas the nature of the agreement and of its collective products is best indicated by the term *communis* and its derivatives. These terms indicate a shared awareness of certain interests that surpass any individual's powers of action and that thus require the voluntary pooling of material and moral resources. One such interest was peace, in the name of which an archbishop of Arles in the twelfth century acknowledged by charter the right of the men of the town to administer themselves by means of twelve "consuls": "This consulate will bring about peace, the re-turn to the good times of old, the reestablishment of society. The churches, the monasteries, and all the holy places consecrated to God; the streets and the public roads; the waters and the land—all shall be governed by this peace. The peace will be sworn for the duration of fifty years, and every five all strangers and newcomers will swear to respect it."[5]

Significant as it was, the institutional feat of creating a collective *potens* through voluntary agreement had to be backed by military might. To assert and defend the franchises they enjoyed, the towns disposed of two significant military resources: city walls and other fortifications, and the urban militia. Though the former were pure-ly defensive, the latter could be used for either defensive or of-fensive purposes; both were sustained by the towns' growing eco-nomic strength.

But just as the typical member of a town militia was not a pro-fessional soldier, so the typical townsman was not primarily and continuously involved in political pursuits, or dependent on them for his total socioeconomic position. Rather, what drew the towns-men together and tied them into a division of labor more complex and dynamic than that known in the countryside were commercial and productive interests; and it was chiefly to construct a context of rule and a juridical environment that would make possible and profitable the conduct of trade and the practice of crafts that the towns sought political autonomy and military self-sufficiency. This is a further novelty with respect to the territorial rulers and the feudal element, for both of which leadership, the exercise of rule, and the practice of governance constituted the original vocation, the focus of their identity and of their mode of life. Even their strong and demanding economic interests were in principle ori-ented to the pursuit of that vocation, the maintenance of that way of life, and found expression in a mode of production where com-mand and coercion played a direct economic role.

The townsmen, on the other hand, demanded the right to rule no one but themselves, and even then only insofar as required for the elaboration and safeguarding of a mode of life revolving around acquisitive and productive pursuits—not the practice of leadership and the experience of war. Yet this very demand posed a challenge the feudal system of rule could not meet. Over the centuries, the feudal element (and, subordinately, the village communities) had developed a vast and complex body of juridical rules focused on land. These rules regulated land tenure, the social groups settled on the land, and the ways those groups exploited it. They ordered the village, the parish, the rural household, and the use of forest, pasture, and common lands; they dealt with *corvée* and *censive*, seigneurial rights and villagers' rights. But at best such a body of rules could encompass the fair and the local market as adjuncts to the manorial economy; its principles could not be made to yield those rules now required by the new, town-based economy, with its accentuated division of labor, its new skills and tools of production, and its new ways of entering into and carrying out transactions and of managing commercial undertakings. A prime concern manifested in early town charters—and in other constitutional documents either bestowed by the ruler or autonomously produced by the towns—was the creation of a distinctive juridical space "immune" from the substantive and procedural rules characteristic of the feudal system. For instance, the settlement of legal disputes through judicial duels was prohibited; courts operating outside the town were forbidden to claim jurisdiction over townsmen; town dwellings were proclaimed inviolable; and above all the juridical status of free men was granted to all townsmen, and often extended to all those who resided in the town for a year and a day (*Stadtluft macht frei*).[6]

But note that the distinctive economic interests of the towns' component socioeconomic groups placed the towns in a complex and almost contradictory position with regard to the problem of rule. For though towns might be juridically and politically autonomous, they were so within a wider context of rule that might be modified to accommodate them but that could not be dispensed with; indeed, it was not in their interest to challenge and "break" that wider context to the extent of becoming self-standing, sovereign political entities. In other words, the "classical" route, leading to the formation of city-states, was not the one the Western medieval towns typically traveled. (Most significant exceptions occurred in Italy.)

The main reason for the existence of this complex situation was that the division of labor I have insisted was characteristic of the town's internal economy presupposed, and was inscribed within, a wider division of labor between town and countryside in which the latter supplied the former with population, food, and raw materials, and in turn absorbed the town's products. Furthermore, a division of labor developed even among the towns themselves: traffic flowed not just between each town and its countryside, but also to and from other towns and other regions.

Over these wide spaces, though, frameworks of rule wider than those the towns themselves could autonomously develop and operate were necessary. In response to this need, towns that were individually powerful mostly banded together not so much to dispense with the wider framework of feudal rule already in existence as to shape its structures and policies in order to make it more amenable to their interests. The best case in point is that of the "sworn alliance" the towns of the county of Flanders entered into when Count Charles the Good was assassinated in 1127 leaving no heir, and on one side the more powerful barons, and on the other the richer and more powerful towns (Bruges, Ghent, Ypres, Lille, and a few others) operated to settle the question of the succession and to establish the terms on which the new count was to rule. Dhondt comments:

At bottom, the rationale for the formation of these alliances (both the barons' and the towns') is to exercise influence on the choice of the new count. And why should barons and towns seek a say on this matter? Obviously on the count will depend the county's general policy. Whether he will be weak or authoritative; whether he will turn primarily toward France or toward England; whether he will favor the towns or support the claims of the knights—these are all extremely concrete problems, and the county's different socioeconomic groups have a stake in their several and distinct implications. To impinge upon the choice of the count entails in fact a means, however primitive, of impinging upon the county's general policy.[7]

Generally speaking, the towns' interests were favored the wider and more uniform the context of rule within which they operated —at any rate insofar as it fell upon that context to police the traffic, to provide a reliable coinage, to enforce market transactions, etc. This is why, between the two forces whose relations defined the feudal system of rule—the territorial ruler and the feudal powers— the towns tended to favor the former.

But the complexity of the towns' political interests could not find expression only in their maneuverings between the dominant forces in the existing political environment. New structures had to be generated that would give the towns, in addition to their political autonomy, the right to participate effectively and permanently in the management of the wider system of rule. The *Stände*— the distinctive late-medieval assemblies, parliaments, diets, estate bodies, and so forth associated with the ruler in the governance of the territory (or individual parts of it)—were the most significant such structures. They did not, of course, involve only the towns; indeed, the clergy and the feudal element had formal precedence in such institutions over the towns. But progressively the feudal element itself gained a *corporate* identity through, and for the purposes of, participation in these structures; and to the extent that this was the case, the feudatories' own relationships to the rulers began to differ from the typical feudal relation of vassal to lord, or lord to suzerain (as we shall see below). And this difference largely conveys the destructive impact that the rise of the towns had on the feudal system of rule.

Stand, Stände, and Ständestaat

It was the entry of the towns into politics, the shift in the balance of power between the territorial ruler and the feudatories in favor of the former, and the change in the terms and structures of the feudal element's participation in the wider system of rule that marked the rise of the Ständestaat. In my view, the Ständestaat was a distinctive, novel, and historically unique system of rule.[8]* Let us discuss its makeup.

To begin with, the term *Stand*, like the broadly equivalent English "estate," has a sociological meaning indicating a specific kind of stratification unit, as in the following statement by T. H. Marshall: "An estate may be defined as a group of people having the same status, in the sense in which that word is used by lawyers. A status in this sense is a position to which is attached a bundle of rights and duties, privileges and obligations, legal capacities and incapacities, which are publicly recognized and which can be defined and enforced by public authority and in many cases by courts of law."[9] Now a group of this kind necessarily possesses some political significance, for the fact that it enjoys certain advantages or suffers from certain disadvantages has been publicly recognized. Within the historical context of my argument, this political significance was increased by the fact that estates were not so much entitled to claim from an outside power an authoritative and if necessary coercive guarantee of their distinctive socioeconomic position (monopolies of skills, exclusive patterns of consumption, etc.) as empowered themselves to issue and enforce rules concerning their own members' rights and obligations, and to prohibit or redress the encroachment by outsiders upon their specific advantages.

However, these political implications were not directly significant for the wider system of rule, the evolving Ständestaat. The latter involved not the existence of "estates" in the above sense, but the operation of "Estates," Stände, constituted bodies devised for the specific purpose of confronting and cooperating with the ruler. These bodies were seen as capable of a peculiar political alchemy whereby the petty political prerogatives of the individual component estates were fused and transformed into more significant claims and wider prerogatives. By assembling into constituted bodies, the Stände represented themselves to the territorial ruler as prepared to associate with him in those aspects of rule that were understood as characteristically public and general. *This* is what makes the Ständestaat into a distinctive system of rule—not the patchwork of corporate groups each empowered to exercise rule, within its own sphere, over its own members and occasionally over third parties. After all, such groups simply paralleled and complemented the individual *potentes* who already exercised such faculties under the feudal dispensation. In the Ständestaat, powerful individuals and groups gathered more or less frequently, personally or through delegates, into variously constituted assemblies and there dealt with the ruler or his agents, voiced their protests, restated their rights, formulated their advice, established the terms of their collaboration with the ruler, and shouldered their share of the burdens of rule.

The typical Ständestaat had a variety of such assemblies that differed in their boundaries (they were always translocal but often provincial or regional rather than territory-wide), in the frequency with which they assembled, in the forms of their deliberations, and in the specific prerogatives they claimed.[10] Furthermore, a Ständestaat might also include constituted bodies that were not, properly speaking, assemblies, but that possessed a more continuous existence than the *ständisch** assemblies and operated differently from them. Such bodies were less directly connected with one or more estates as their socioeconomic constitutency; examples included universities, large religious foundations, and in France and adjacent territories *Parlements*, i.e., learned, semiprofessional judicial bodies.

Let us take as an example of a mature Ständestaat the arrangements for rule in the Franche-Comté in the first part of the sixteenth century. At that time, the Franche-Comté was a province of the Holy Roman Empire, and thus under the rulership of the Hapsburg Emperor Charles V. He was an absentee prince, however, and ruled through personal representatives; moreover, he allowed the Comté to preserve its ständisch structures of rule well

---

* I use the German *ständisch*, since English lacks a comparable adjective form for the word "Estate."

after their equivalents in the French provinces had been considerably run down. In the exercise of rule over the Comté, the emperor's representative and the small body of *bons personnages*
surrounding him found themselves confronted *and* associated with
two independent, ständisch power centers: a Parlement, and the
Estates.

The first held regular and lengthy sessions in Dôle. It had
about 25 members, the majority of whom were trained in law,
since the Parlement's primary function was to serve as an appeals
court. By the sixteenth century, however, the Parlement's competence had been extended to include the regular supervision of
all other, lesser judicial bodies; and additional prerogatives, more
clearly of an administrative nature, had been successfully claimed.
For example, the Parlement had established its rights to demand
reports from the agents of the ruler, to send its members to ascer-
tain matters of public concern regarding the territory, and to mandate urgent action on those matters. As a result, "everything was
paraded in front of the counselors making up the Parlement: questions of general security, of criminality, of heresy; the various
aspects of rural life; the regulation of pastures, hunting, and fish-
ing, and of forests, meadows, and vineyards; the control over
crafts; the maintenance of roads, bridges, and [navigation on] rivers; the revision of tolls; the maintenance of a uniform currency;
the policing of fairs and markets; the export of salt, iron, wine, and
wheat; and the prices of meals at inns." On all these matters "the
Parlement decided everything, alone, as a sovereign." It constituted "a collective governor, strong in its traditions, in the favor of
the prince, and in its immortality."[11]

The Estates of the Comté had three chambers—of the clergy, the
nobility, and the towns. The members of the first two Estates were
entitled to take part personally in the proceedings of their chambers; the third chamber was composed mainly of the towns' mayors
and high office-holders, including judges. "The three chambers deliberate separately, form their own internal resolutions by majority
vote, and deal with one another through deputies. Their rights are

the same."[12] The chief prerogatives of the Estates were financial. Though considerable, the revenues the ruler drew from his own domains in the Franche-Comté did not suffice to reward his representatives and agents and to finance the discharging of his own tasks of governance. Since the Comté prided itself on not being subject to regular taxes, the ruler's representatives had to ask the Estates to supplement those revenues by granting periodically a "noncompulsory subsidy" (*don gratuit*).

Over the years the Estates had learned to make excellent use of this prerogative. Though they did not really feel at liberty to deny the ruler his request, normally in granting it they reserved to themselves the right to make arrangements for the levy to finance it: the amount to be levied and the means of collection; the apportionment of the burden among the Comté's three bailiwicks; and the procedure for considering objections. To oversee all these matters they appointed from among themselves a nine-man commission responsible for the entire operation. Furthermore, "since they decided on the tax and controlled its exaction, the Estates, little by little and as a matter of course, came to exercise a supervision upon its expenditure."[13] At each session, they presented to the ruler their claims, which they expected would be treated as statements of the needs and demands of the territory, and thus as directives for the ruler's administrative action.

To counter the resulting restrictions on his freedom of action, the ruler, through his power to summon the Estates, tried to make their sessions shorter and less frequent, and had them addressed on his behalf by influential spokesmen. The Parlement, too, opposed the Estates' claims when they seemed to encroach upon its own prerogatives.

Dualism as a Structural Principle

To simplify the argument, I shall consider in this section only the Estates as the ruler's associates in rule, leaving aside such relatively specialized bodies as the Parlements. As we have seen, the Estates were assemblies, gatherings of individually or corporatively powerful elements. How, then, did they differ, from a constitutional viewpoint, from those assemblies of the feudal period in which the feudatories gathered to offer their counsel to their lord?[14] Apart from the fact that the Estates included also the clergy and the towns, there were three main differences. First, a gathering of the feudal barons was generally a more ad hoc affair than a session of the Estates; where the former operated with competences and decision procedures mostly vaguely determined by custom, the latter generally operated under detailed, written rules stating how deliberations were to be conducted within each chamber, how they were to be made known "across chambers," and how they were to be merged into the collective Estates' decisions and communicated to the ruler.

Second, in a baronial gathering the spread-out network of linkages connecting a lord and his vassals, at various removes, was "pulled in" and concentrated, as it were; however, this did not alter its essential nature as an elaborate complex of *personal* connections between powerful individuals. A feudal assembly remained in principle one of persons who were singly *potentes*, and who together, to use again Theodor Mayer's expression, made up "the state as an association of persons." The constituted ständisch bodies, on the other hand, had a more or less explicit *territorial* reference; they were, as indicated above, gatherings of the Estates of a territory—whether province, *pays*, county, principality, country, *Land*, or realm—understood as a unit with identifiable physical boundaries.[15*]

Third, a typical feudal gathering served not so much to *confront* the ruler with his barons as to *condense* them around him, for the barons tended to see the ruler more as an overlord or suzerain, and thus as a *primus inter pares*, than as the current occupant of a distinctively public office. The typical assembly of Estates, however, stood over against the ruler, represented the territory to him. Implicitly, such an assembly of Estates recognized and asserted the peculiarity of the ruler's position vis-à-vis the territory that they embodied.

These three aspects distinguishing the ständisch bodies from feudal gatherings characterize the Ständestaat as a whole, since ständisch bodies were the most distinctive component of the new rule system. In short, then, the Ständestaat differed from the feudal system essentially in being more *institutionalized* in its operations, in having an explicit *territorial* reference, and in being *dualistic*, since it confronted the ruler with the Stände and associated the two elements in rule as distinct power centers.

This last notion—of the "dualism" of the Ständestaat—has been much emphasized in the literature since its formulation in the nineteenth century by the great German jurist Otto von Gierke. It suggests that the territorial ruler and the Stände make up the polity jointly, but as separate and mutually acknowledged political centers. Both constitute it, through their mutual agreement;[16] but even during the agreement's duration they remain distinct, each exercising powers of its own, and differing in this from the "organs" of the mature, "unitary" modern state (see Chapter 5 below). That the Stände would address problems of rule as partners, as self-standing possessors of rights and faculties, not as submissive dependents, is apparent from the following passage, in which the chronicler of the French Estates General of 1357 reports the speech of Robert Le Coq, bishop of Laon and the Estates' chief spokesman for "reform":

He said that lately the King and the kingdom had been poorly governed, whence many ills had come both to the kingdom and its inhabitants, in particular through modifications in the coinage and through levies, as well as bad administration and government of the moneys the King had received from the people; out of these moneys very considerable amounts had been given, oftentimes, to some who had not deserved them. And all these things, said the bishop, had been done upon the counsel of the chancellor and of others, as well as of others again who had in the past governed the King. The bishop said further that the people could no longer tolerate such things; and to this end they had deliberated jointly that the officials mentioned below . . . are to be deprived in perpetuity of all royal offices. . . . *Item*, the same bishop also requested that the officials of the Kingdom of France be suspended and that reformers be appointed, to be nominated by the three Estates;

such reformers are to have cognizance of anything they choose to demand of the above officials.[17]

The success of this constitutional initiative of the Estates General was only temporary. But even much later documents from this and other bodies, in France and elsewhere, attest to the Stände's insistence on their role as independent powers. At the same time, one must stress that it was as the two halves of a single system of rule that the Stände and the ruler came together. Together they generated, as it were, a single "field of rule" traversed by a unitary political process that had its poles in both. Clearly, to be made compatible with and conducive to such unity, the dualism of the Ständestaat had to be filtered through institutional arrangements much more sophisticated and complex than those characteristic of the feudal system. To this extent, the dualism called forth, and was tempered by, another characteristic mentioned above—the new system's high degree of institutionalization. We shall return to this later.[18]

Let us turn for the moment to the relation between the Ständestaat's dualism (in Gierke's sense) and its other characteristic mentioned above—its territoriality. Estates stood over against the ruler, as I have said, in that they represented the territory to him; they either recognized and complemented him specifically in his capacity as territorial ruler, or they reminded him of his proper role.[19] According to Carsten, this last function was particularly significant in the rise to power of the Estates in Germany. In the late Middle Ages, the numerous rulers of the German lands engaged in dynastic-patrimonial policies that led to their lands being sold, partitioned, mortgaged, or overrun—with ruinous effects on their subjects. In several German territories the Estates first gathered and began to function in order to resist and moderate such policies. They saw themselves as embodying "the people of the territory," and in this capacity they could strengthen considerably one dynasty's claim to rule against another's. Moreover, they could and did use this power to assert the unity of each territory and to share in its rule.[20]

But the fact that in a variety of circumstances the Stände, in Germany and elsewhere, put themselves forward as embodying or representing "the people" or "the territory" or both, and in this capacity dualistically confronted the ruler and cooperated with him, should not conceal a different meaning of "dualism." The Ständestaat, like the feudal system before it and the absolutist system after it, was also dualistic in the wider sense of excluding the great majority of the population from any political significance. Insofar as they claimed and exercised an exclusive right to conduct the business of rule jointly, both the territorial ruler and the Estates made up the *same* pole of this wider dualism. The apparent fragmentation of sovereignty among a number of individual and collective subjects of rule in the Ständestaat; the often strained relations between the Estates and the prince; the different packages of rights and privileges, including those of rule and self-rule, to which different groups could lay claim—these things should not blind us to the fact that the whole system rested economically and politically on the backs of a voiceless, oppressed majority. The Estates "represented" the interests of the people and the territory only to the extent that they could identify those interests as their own, as those of a privileged minority. The *meliores terrae* saw themselves as *being* the territory. Yet when assembled in the Estates they represented no one but themselves; they voiced, and stood on, their own rights.

Of course, because their livelihood rested ultimately on the toil of the populace, the *meliores* often found it in their interest to protest and intervene on behalf of the people—to protect them against raids and looting by feuding lords, against the depredations of mercenary troops billeted in the countryside, against the ravages of "pestilence, famine, and war," against the greed of unscrupulous churchmen, and against the levying of extortionate taxes by rulers. Besides, there were also other, *moral* bonds between this or that privileged minority and the section of the populace it somehow "incorporated." But, politically speaking, the great majority of the population appeared not as constituents of or participants in the system of rule, but merely as the objects of rule.

Here, then, "dualism" meant that the populace—still mostly settled on land in a variety of subaltern statuses, and enclosed within exacting and encompassing relations of dependence on their "betters"—relied on the political activity of those "betters" to safeguard their interests. And their interests could be voiced and upheld in properly political terms—that is, other than through short-lived insurrections, city riots, desertion of villages, and so forth —only insofar as they coincided with those of one or another of the privileged Stände, which would then try to assert them through the appropriate constituted body.

The Component Groups

We have examined two elements of dualism distinctive to the Ständestaat system—the relations between Stände and ruler, and between joint rulers and ruled. To burden the term "dualism" still further, one might suggest that each of the two key components of the Estates system, the feudal element and the town element, was involved in rule "dually": each exercised rule within the narrow compass of its own autonomy (the governance and exploitation of the "immune" fief; the internal government of the "chartered" town), and each also exercised rule over a larger territorial unit through the Estates.

The political process in the Ständestaat largely revolved around issues on which the feudal and town elements were at loggerheads, and on which each was engaged with the other *and* with the ruler in a momentous, three-cornered power struggle. In this section I shall discuss this struggle solely by characterizing its principals. Let us begin with the ruler.

In turning again to Gierke's notion of the Ständestaat's dualism, we should note that the two parties, Stände and ruler, were not on the same plane. As in the feudal relation, there was enough closeness between the parties in the ständisch "compact of rule" to make it morally binding and mutually honorable. But again as in the feudal relation, there was an asymmetry between the parties, and it favored the ruler. Furthermore, in this context the ruler's superiority was not of a feudal nature, that of an overlord or suzerain, but of a distinctively public, territorial, regalian nature. Of course, conspicuous legacies of feudalism persisted in the ruler's position. He was still typically the *seigneur* of large domains, on which he relied as far as possible to support his household and finance his policies. And, as we have seen in the case of German lands, some ruling dynasties still attached a largely patrimonial significance to the entire territories they ruled, not just to their seigneurial domains. By and large, however, the ruler increasingly operated, and the Stände envisaged him, as the holder of the nonfeudal, public title of king, prince, or duke. As such he stood above the Estates, though they were his associates in rule. "The prince was ruler *before* the compact, *without* the compact."[21] Powerful individuals or bodies might relate to him still in feudal terms; but the Stände perforce addressed him in terms that acknowledged him as sovereign, as the embodiment of a higher, more compelling majesty and right. To the ruler so envisaged the Estates corporately offered, on the compact's terms, both their support and their resistance.

Since this last phenomenon—the Estates' resistance—is often emphasized in discussions of their role,[22] it should be made clear, first, that the resistance in question was legitimate (involving, as I suggested above, the Estates' "standing on their rights") and, second, that the Estates arose very often on the initiative of the ruler himself in his search for financial support. For as the revenues from the ruler's seigneurial domains became inadequate to meet his commitments and support his undertakings—especially his military ones— he turned to the feudal elements and the towns and urged them to constitute themselves into Estate assemblies so that he might gain access, with their consent, to economic resources to which he had otherwise no legitimate claim. Of course, the Estates bartered their consent in return for a claim to direct the attendant fiscal operations themselves. Sometimes, as in the case of the Franche-Comté, they even claimed control over the expenditure of the resulting yield. But this was a necessary and not exorbitant price for the ruler to pay—after all, the Stände operated their administrative arrangements at no cost to him.

This connection between the ruler's needs and the rise of the Estates is sometimes proved *a contrario* by the circumstances of the Estates's "withering away" with the advent of absolutist rule. In Prussia, in particular, the key move in the ruler's drive toward absolutism was the creation (with the initial consent of the Estates) of a new tax, the urban excise on consumption goods; the administration of this tax was placed in the hands not of the Estates but of an apparatus under the ruler's personal control, and the resulting revenue was directed chiefly to the establishment and maintenance of the ruler's standing army. Having thus bypassed the Estates both in commandeering a fiscal flow and in putting it to military use, the ruler increasingly was able to dispense with their support and ignore their resistance.[23]

It is perhaps worth making explicit at this point that "the ruler" in the previous argument cannot realistically be taken solely as the physical person of the current head of a ruling dynasty. For immediately around the ruler so understood, wholly sharing his interests and seeking their assertion, stood normally not just his extended family but also a large household of familiars and dependents who were not his kin but who were sometimes close, trusted, and much-rewarded associates. Progressively, this household became the center of a new, even larger body of political-administrative personnel all of whose members, however exalted and handsomely rewarded, stood in a relation of greater dependence on and submission to the ruler than was ever the case with feudal vassalage.[24]

One may distinguish within this body of personnel three categories (which sometimes overlapped): clerics, university-trained lawyers, and nobles seeking preferment at court. They all served the ruler as his personal appointees and delegates rather than as independent holders of jurisdictional prerogatives. They bore titles that often revealed the lowly household origin of functions now becoming dignified and respectable. They were supported either directly from the ruler's purse or indirectly from the revenues associated with their titles or from other patrimonial arrangements often formalized in feudal terms. They were the ruler's servants in rule—his envoys abroad, the heads of his emergent administrative units, the members of his closer councils, his advocates before the Stände, the judges in his courts, and the leaders of his armies. With their aid, the ruler was able to pursue the peculiar dynamic mission of the nascent modern state: the achievement of sovereignty both externally (vis-à-vis the emperor, the pope, or other rulers with claims upon the territory), and internally (vis-à-vis the feudal magnates and, increasingly, the Stände).

If we turn to the feudal element, we clearly observe a split within the manifold faculties of rule they exercised. On the one hand, at the local level individual feudatories went on exercising most of their traditional jurisdictional powers over the rural population. But increasingly these powers were valued for the contribution they made to the economic well-being of the individual feudal lineages, to the maintenance of their exalted social position—in short, to the "private" interests of these noble rentiers. On the other hand, at a higher, translocal level participation in the ständisch bodies had become the main mode of political activity for the feudal element just as it had for other privileged groups. Here the feudatories operated as a corporate entity, vesting rights in individuals (or lineages, rather) in their capacity as members of such bodies, not as singly powerful *particuliers*. In this sense, we can say that the feudal element had learned the towns' lesson in the corporate exercise of political power. The more ambitious feudatories, however, had a further avenue to power (and often wealth): they could enter the circle of close advisers and companions most rulers built around themselves, and whose members they often selected from among the feudal magnates.

With the towns, too, we can see a split between the local and translocal levels of political activity. Though at neither level were powers of rule vested in principle in individuals as such (unless we count among such powers those of a patriarchal nature exercised by family heads over urban households), and though even locally individuals exercised rule as holders of corporate offices, some of those offices were monopolized from early on by strong corporate subgroups (economically dominant crafts or trades), and some were begining to be absorbed into the patrimonies of wealthy urban lineages. Similar "oligarchic" and "plutocratic" trends can be detected at the translocal level with reference to the question of who should represent the town in the Estate assemblies. Within individual towns, these trends were occasionally interrupted by reversions toward broadly based popular government.

It is noteworthy that the town polities provided a setting for experimentation with new political, administrative, and legal arrangements that progressively penetrated the wider context of rule. In particular, the growing size of the towns, and the fact that the distinctively urban social groups were committed primarily to economic pursuits, as I mentioned earlier, led to the formation of elected representative bodies that often "governed" by enacting statutes—a momentous innovation. Complementary to these bodies, and formally dependent on them, there came to be established specifically political roles with differentiated competences and requirements for occupancy; they were conceived as separate from the person of their appointed or elected occupants, who were charged with attending continuously to political business. Also, it was at the level of city politics that secular literati and university-trained lawyers came forward in large numbers to serve as a new type of political-administrative personnel.[25]*

I have already stressed that in the Ständestaat the great majority of the population appeared purely as the objects of rule. Nonetheless, toward the end of the feudal period rural populations in various places had experimented with means of generating politically effective solidarities between powerless equals. Their results, as we have seen, were later put to good, "aggressive" use by town populations; but in the countryside their aims had been largely defen-

55

sive, with the initiative and leadership mainly coming from the clergy and the chief outcomes being temporary "leagues" intended to protect the rural peace from breaches by feuding barons. Though these rural experiments were an important component in the transition from the feudal to the ständisch system of rule,[26] once the latter was established the political significance of such initiatives among the rural population became marginal. At the local level there still existed rural communities claiming distinctive rights for their members; but the organs of such communities operated intermittently, for the most part, and were expected to limit their activities to voicing complaints about violations of the communities' rights to the ruler or the relevant ständisch bodies, who would provide a remedy against prevaricating seigneurs or encroaching towns. The situation of those urban lower strata who, unable to monopolize skills or tools, could find no place in the town's internal system of estates was in a sense worse, for they could not even appeal in defense of their interests to ancient customs, as the rural populace often could.

The Political Legacy of the Ständestaat

We have seen that the constituent elements of the Ständestaat were preeminently interested in questions of privileges and rights: rights of the ruler as against those of the Stände, and vice versa; or the respective rights of each estate vis-à-vis the others. On this point there was an essential continuity between the Ständestaat and the feudal system of rule. For example, it is noteworthy that the estates' differentiated rights were often designated "liberties," a concept whose basic meaning had much to do with the ancient notion of "immunity."[27] But there were significant differences between the two systems, too.

Forcible redress of violated rights by those claiming the rights ("self-help") became less frequent under the Ständestaat system, as the ruler, acting often on protests against the penchant of feudatories for plundering and massacring one another's dependents as a way of asserting their own contested rights, came to hedge armed self-help with conditions and restrictions and showed himself ready and able to visit his own wrath on any transgressors. In various territories, too, rulers established systems of courts to deal out justice on the basis of their own new, "learned" law.

Thus both the normal exercise and the occasional reassertion of rights (even rights of rule) became less rough-and-ready, less openly coercive and threatening to the security of order, more literate and legalistic. Much political business now involved taking and giving advice prior to giving and enforcing commands; consulting interested parties, official documents, and qualified authorities; and reaching decisions, or voicing objections to or reservations about decisions, on stated grounds. In these largely novel modalities of the political process (often brutally interrupted by straightforward aggression, usurpation, or repression) we can see prefigured the predominantly discursive, businesslike temper of the internal political processes of the modern state. Finally, since much of the controversy about rights now revolved not around feudal relations but around the respective "public" prerogatives of the ruler and of the Stände, it was increasingly carried out in the language of learned law, Roman and canon, rather than in that of "barbaric," customary law and the folk jural tradition. Again, this contributed to "civilizing" the political process in the sense just suggested.

The above indications concern the modalities, the forms of the political process. Its content was mainly generated on the one hand by the ruler-Stände relation and on the other by the crosscutting relationships between the territorial ruler, the feudal element, and the town-based groups. As I have repeatedly indicated, these three shared an unchallenged, politically unproblematical supremacy over the mass of the population; but their interests, the cultural and economic bases of each group's social power, differed enough to generate sustained conflict among them. Alignments among the parties varied according to the issues. For instance, once the towns had stabilized their relations with the surrounding rural economies, the town estates came to share the feudal element's resistance to the ruler's policies intended to spread his control uniformly over the whole territory; townsmen and feudatories together sought to uphold local or regional traditions and autonomy. At the same time, the distinctive status concerns and cultural physiognomy of both the feudatories and the ruling dynasties as components of a landed noble class brought them together in shared opposition to the economic and status advances of the urban groups.

Despite a variety of crisscrossing alignments among the three protagonists, there was a broad tendency for the urban groups, once they had gained a legitimate position within the system of rule, to support the territorial ruler's drive to restrict the political significance of the feudal element. They did so by lending him their financial and military support and, increasingly, by manning his growing administrative apparatus. This basic trend interacts in various ways (1) with other tendencies, particularly the rulers' rejection of effective subordination to the emperor or the pope, and sometimes the king, and (2) with the shifting military and diplomatic equilibrium between territorial rulers.

Böckenförde has provided a useful summary of the most significant outcomes for Western history of the manifold conflicts and accommodations that resulted from this interaction.[28] In France, one territorial ruling dynasty progressively centralized power and politically weakened the Estates, building up an increasingly effective apparatus of rule around the monarch. In England, a monarchy that had started from a very strong position in the twelfth and thirteenth centuries met with progressively stronger opposition from the Estates. At length, after the fall of the Stuarts, the centralizing drive continued—but with Parliament as its focus. In Germany, centralization was carried out at comparatively low levels by territorial rulers who successfully opposed attempts by higher-level forces to make the Empire itself a state. In most parts of Germany, the failure of high-level centralization meant that the establishment of strong political-administrative structures of rule was retarded at all levels. The main exception was Prussia.

For the purposes of our typological treatment, the French and the (later) Prussian outcomes are more significant than the English one because they best embody the absolutist system of rule, our subject in the next chapter.

CHAPTER IV

The Absolutist System of Rule

IN THE LAST CHAPTER, I suggested that the rise of towns in the medieval West sharply differentiated the social, economic, and cultural context of the emerging Ständestaat from that of the preceding feudal system of rule. No equally dramatic contextual change suggests itself as having been significantly associated with the transition to the absolutist system of rule between the seventeenth and eighteenth centuries in such countries as France, Spain, Prussia, and Austria. Instead, I think that this "type switch" is best related to a new set of specifically *political* demands and opportunities confronting the existing systems of rule. From this perspective, the dynamic causing the shift operated not so much within each state considered in isolation as within the *system* of states. The strengthening of territorial rule and the absorption of smaller and weaker territories into larger and stronger ones—processes that had gone on throughout the historical career of the Ständestaat— led to the formation of a relatively small number of mutually independent states, each defining itself as sovereign and engaged with the others in an inherently open-ended, competitive, and risk-laden power struggle.

This largely novel pattern of relationships among larger political entities (to be discussed further in the next chapter) placed a considerable premium on a state's ability to tighten its internal political ordering, to structure rule so as to make it more unitary, continuous, calculable, and effective. If a given state were to hold or improve its position vis-à-vis others, one center within it would increasingly have to monopolize rule over its territory, exercising that rule with the least possible mediation and intervention of other centers outside its own control. Each state would also have to perfect tools of government to transmit promptly, uniformly, and reliably the center's will throughout the territory, and to mobilize as required the relevant resources of the society. Thus the new tensions, threats, and challenges that each sovereign state generated and confronted externally heightened and favored the territorial ruler's drive to gather unto himself all powers of rule—a drive already visible and significant within the Ständestaat—until a qualitatively different system of rule came into being internally.[1] On the other hand, though still emphasizing the *political* determinants of this phenomenon, we may order the relations between its internal and external aspects the other way around: we may treat as the *primum mobile* the ruler's drive for more effective and exclusive rule, and see the mutually defiant, self-centered posture of all states toward one another as the result rather than the cause of that drive.[2]

However we choose between these two constructions, we should also note that the development of absolutist rule was favored, and perhaps made inevitable, by other internal political phenomena— one example being the necessity of curbing the warlike confrontations that occurred between religious-political factions within a single territory in the aftermath of the Reformation. In fact, an Italian scholar has placed the end of the French Ständestaat around 1614–15 and has traced its cause to the shock engendered by the assassination of Henri IV by a religious fanatic in 1610.[3] Finally, the accelerating commercialization of the economy, the result both of the inner dynamic of the city-based productive system (now irresistibly moving toward the establishment of the capitalist mode of production) and of the bullion flowing into Europe from overseas, also played a significant role in the transition to absolutism. However, my main concern in this chapter is not to go into complex questions of causes but simply to describe the demise of the Ständestaat and to characterize the new, absolutist system of rule, which is widely considered the first mature embodiment of the modern state.

The Towns and the Decline of the Ständestaat

In 1629, Cardinal Richelieu wrote in a summary of the main directives of royal policy he was addressing to his master, Louis XIII: "Reduce and restrict those bodies which, because of pretensions to sovereignty, always oppose the good of the realm. Ensure that your majesty is absolutely obeyed by great and small."[4] The target envisaged here was primarily the higher nobility, and its resistance required several decades of purposeful and relentless policy to overcome. But the ruthlessly dynamic character of that policy is indicated by the fact that among its later targets were bodies—such as the Paris Parlement, largely composed of ennobled bourgeois elements—that previously had strongly supported royal power against the feudal nobility. It was not only the nobility whose faculties of rule were progressively confiscated by the advance of absolutism.

But the open clash between the monarch and the Estates is only the most visible and dramatic part of the story. I want to argue that the Estates' resistance was also, and largely, weakened from within, that social and economic developments deprived them of the will and the ability to play an independent political role either as the opponents of royal power or as its partners. For reasons largely internal to their constituencies, the upper, public, properly political layers of the Estates' jurisdictional prerogatives had effectively ceased to operate before they were taken away. Let us see how this happened, beginning with the urban element.

As I suggested previously, the interests that had led urban groups to seek political autonomy and to participate in the ständisch constituted bodies had been not specifically political ones, expressing an inherent vocation to rule, but rather commercial and productive ones, seeking a political guarantee. The predominant intent of the towns' original political efforts had been twofold: on the one hand, to obtain formal recognition of their internal articulation into privileged, corporate groupings; and on the other hand, to construct *with* the ruler and the feudal element, through the Estates, wider frameworks for law enforcement and order-keeping conducive to the security and progress of their business pursuits.

Both objectives had been achieved. But the territorial ruler had played an increasingly preponderant part in securing the second through his use of a fiscal, military, and administrative apparatus dependent on him alone (though often manned by personnel of bourgeois extraction). Nonetheless, the dominant urban groups felt satisfied with this fact. Indeed, they thought it best to rely on further extensions and elaborations of the ruler's faculties of rule as a response to the remaining perturbations of "law and order," which now, since the feudal element had been denied the right to engage in feuds and private wars, originated from other challenges to the ruler's sovereignty in the form of religious dissension and interstate conflict. So far as such groups were concerned, the ruler could ensure the construction and upkeep of increasingly large, uniform, and territory-wide frameworks for the regulation and support of urban economic activities in a way that no other body— not even the ständisch bodies, with their prevalently regional bases —could do. From the standpoint of the emergent system of international law, too, the ruler was in a unique position to protect and further the wealthier town groups' growing interest in the expansion of foreign markets, the exploitation of overseas resources, or the prevention of foreign competition.[5]

Thus, rather than exercise their political (and military) muscle, the towns were willing to renounce most of the powers of the regional or territory-wide constituted bodies.[6]* For that matter, some increasingly significant urban groups were no longer particularly interested in maintaining even the towns' internal autonomy. After all, the corporative regulation of craft production and trade had not kept up with changes in the material and social technology of production and stood in the way of those urban

63

elements eager to use their wealth as capital, to make it yield profits by using it to buy labor power as a commodity. Opportunities of this kind distracted some townsmen from political concerns—obscuring their interests as townsmen or members of specific corporations while heightening their awareness of their purely individual interests as capital owners. For such people, both the town's internal politics and its active participation in the wider system of rule were increasingly becoming a nuisance—again, at least as long as law and order were otherwise maintained.

And the territorial ruler did stand ready to maintain them, and to regulate and sustain old and new productive and commercial pursuits. In its internal aspect, *mercantilism*, the distinctive economic policy of the absolutist regimes, was largely a matter of diminishing the autonomy of locally based organs of economic regulation either by suppressing them or, more often, by integrating them into a uniform, statewide system that was more technically sophisticated, less tradition-bound, and more effectively policed than such local organs had been.[7] For instance, though most guild and craft groupings remained in operation, they did so as police organs working under elaborate rules now issued by the sovereign. In France, edicts of François II and Charles IX, dating from 1560 and 1563, respectively, suppressed the independent merchants' courts and turned their jurisdiction over to the state judicial system; but former members of the suppressed courts were co-opted as assessors into the state ones. Ordinances promulgated by the French kings to regulate business relations often derived much of their content from statutes and customs that merchants and tradesmen had previously elaborated for their own use and had autonomously enforced.[8]

The vitality and autonomy (and the credibility, as we might say today) of the urban political institutions were further diminished by bitter internal rivalries that had developed over particular jurisdictional rights and privileges. It had become possible for an individual or a family to obtain from the ruler an exclusive, hereditary entitlement to this or that fragment of the town's corporate prerogatives, to this or that fiscal exemption or honorific privilege; this meant, as I suggested in the last chapter, that distinctive urban rights were losing their corporate nature and becoming absorbed within the patrimonies of individual "patrician" lineages. But this perverted their nature; prevented their exercise as part of an autonomous, open-ended political process; and above all caused dissensions that paralyzed the town's body politic, and sometimes even the translocal constituted bodies in which the towns were represented.

Visible expressions of the loss of political purpose and potency on the part of the urban element were the competition for ennoblement within the bourgeoisie (in France this led to the establishment of a *noblesse de robe*, which invidiously distanced itself from the commoner urban element without ever being accepted by the feudal *noblesse d'épée* as its peer); the aping of feudal manners by the wealthier bourgeois; and the tracing of more and more conspicuous (and again invidious) lines of status demarcation between adjacent groups within the town's population. Increasingly, economic *class* contrasts played a significant part—if perhaps a less apparent one—in the same process.[9]

The Feudal Element and the Decline of the Ständestaat

As far as the feudal element is concerned, its economic position largely deteriorated over the period we are considering owing to the increasing commercialization of the economy. For instance, the influx of bullion devalued money and thereby decreased in real terms the money revenues of landed groups, which were often fixed. And the honor code of the nobility (sometimes backed by the formal sanction of the loss of noble status) often prevented it from taking full advantage of the opportunities for gain opened up by commercialization.[10] This weakened the feudal element vis-à-vis both the monarch and the bourgeoisie. The richer bourgeois, particularly in France, took advantage of the royal practice of selling certain offices and outbid the nobles for them, thus preempting for themselves the generally lucrative advantages of those offices.

In the face of conspicuous expenditure on the part of wealthier bourgeois, the nobility found it increasingly difficult to maintain their distinctively affluent, leisurely, and honorable style of life. Naturally, this did not make for political understanding and co-operation between the older and the newer privileged groups. Life at the monarch's court came to be seen as a way for the feudal nobility to emphasize its distinctiveness, and moreover could some-times lead to economic gain. But for the most part it was ruinously costly, and it placed the nobility in a position of dependence on the monarch, as we shall see; it also led to the growth of rivalries among the courtiers themselves.

A further problem was that the feudal element had largely lost its military significance, and thus one of its original political tasks. Of course, the military effectiveness of the feudal host proper—a small elite of mounted, heavily armored warriors—had long since been at an end. But for a few centuries afterward the nobility had preserved military functions of other sorts. As part of his general upbringing, the typical nobleman was trained to lead into battle, on behalf of the ruler, small troops of his own dependents. These normally were hastily recruited for relatively short expeditions, and fought an unsophisticated, rough-and-ready kind of warfare, with elementary weapons of their own or supplied to them by their noble leader.

In the new context of interstate politics, however, momentous developments in the material and social technology of warfare had made it imperative that states intending to survive and prosper maintain a standing army, and in relevant cases, a war fleet, both financed, equipped, and officered at the initiative of the ruler.[11] There were several important implications of this new fact of political life: one was that aristocratic ancestry and upbringing no longer in themselves qualified an individual for competent and re-liable military leadership; a second was that warfare in its new form was no longer easily compatible with the maintenance of a noble style of life; a third was that it ceased to be within the means of the average nobleman to equip personally a military unit of the kind now required; and a fourth, following from the third, was that the noble wanting to go on performing military tasks had to do it on new terms—the ruler's.[12]

If we further consider that the ruler's expanded and professionalized system of courts had been making the judicial powers of the feudal element less significant even at the local level, it becomes clear that the nobility simply could not have maintained its previous political leverage, whether through ständisch bodies or through seigneurial powers. Even locally, the traditional rights of rule of the feudatories progressively lost all but their economic and status significance. By avariciously enforcing what rights they still enjoyed, the landed groups went on fighting their rearguard action against the encroaching power of mobile, commercial, moneyed interests, went on seeking to maintain their distinctive, leisurely mode of existence and their social prerogative.

There was an additional way for the feudal element to associate itself with the ruler's political undertakings: individual nobles could attach themselves to the ruler's court and seek to enter his closer councils. But they had to do so on his terrain and again on his terms, not on the former terms of exercising traditional corporate rights and duties of aid and counsel. Any renewed attempt by the feudal element to play a serious political role through the old ständisch bodies was bound to be considered a challenge to the royal power and dealt with accordingly.[13]

The Ruler and His Court: France

I have suggested some powerful long-term trends that undermined the Estates' powers both of effective resistance to the growing hegemony of the ruler and of positive intervention in the business of rule; moreover, I have noted that most of these trends were already at work during the heyday of the Ständestaat. If to these trends not directly of the monarch's making we add his own policies specifically intended to achieve the same end—in France, for instance, the deliberate exclusion of princes of the blood from holding military governorships—we can see how together they eliminated the Ständestaat's characteristic dualism (in Gierke's sense). In the absolutist state the political process is no longer structured primarily by the continuous, legitimate tension and collaboration between two independent centers of rule, the ruler and the Stände; it develops around and from the former only.

In most cases the ständisch constituted bodies were not formally done away with: the French Estates General, for example, were simply not summoned between 1614 and 1789. Many bodies kept "representing" the differentiated packages of rights and immunities of their constituent groups long after they had ceased to play an effective political role.[14] But, I repeat, those rights and immunities they claimed involved *public* powers of rule less and less—except petty ones (fiscal exemptions in particular) that benefited the individuals enjoying them exclusively as components of patrimonies, as counters in the games of mutual disparagement and envy they played with one another. But *rule*—the ability to initiate collective action, to participate in the determination of public policy and supervise its execution, to attend to the needs of the larger society and shape its future—this power the Stände had lost.

Rule now rested solely with the monarch, who had gathered all effective (as against formal) public prerogatives unto himself. To exercise it, he first had to increase his own prominence, had to magnify and project the majesty of his powers by greatly enlarging his court and intensifying its glamour. The absolute ruler's court was no longer the upper section of his household, a circle of relatives, close associates, and favored dependents. It was an extensive, artificially constructed and regulated, highly distinctive world that appeared to outsiders (and to foreigners) to be a lofty plateau, an exalted stage at the center of which the ruler stood in a position of unchallengeable superiority. The ruler's person, to begin with, was continuously displayed in the glare of the condensed and heightened "public" world embodied in the court. Let us consider this phenomenon in the seventeenth-century French court, which best exemplified it. The king of France was thoroughly, without residue, a "public" personage. His mother gave birth to him in public, and from that moment his existence, down to its most trivial moments, was acted out before the eyes of attendants who were holders of dignified offices. He ate in public, went to bed in public, woke up and was clothed and groomed in public, urinated and defecated in public. He did not much bathe in public; but then neither did he do so in private. I know of no evidence that he copulated in public; but he came near enough, considering the circumstances under which he was expected to deflower his august bride. When he died (in public), his body was promptly and messily chopped up in public, and its severed parts ceremoniously handed out to the more exalted among the personages who had been attending him throughout his mortal existence.[15*]

The court around him was so constituted as to magnify and display that existence. It was a visible world of privilege. Its physical settings; the manner and dress of the courtiers; its highly symbolic, ritualized, and wasteful routine—all conveyed an image of splendor, grace, luxury, and leisure. The "lofty plateau," as I have called it, was carefully terraced, building up to the figure of the ruler through multiple, visible gradations—gradations in the courtiers' titles, in their proximity to the ruler, in the frequency and ease of their access to him, in their ceremonial precedences, and in the markings of status encoded in their dress and posture.[16]

Note that this artificial context, with so many characteristics heightening the courtiers' sense of status, perforce made them mutually envious, mistrustful, and hostile. It facilitated the emergence of cabals, intrigues, and furtive and shifting alignments of mutually suspicious associates; it thrived on gossip and spying. Thus the concerns of the courtiers (who often had no choice but to attend court) became focused on issues whose outcomes might be consequential at best for the standing of this or that individual but could not change their shared condition of gilded isolation, dependence, and impotence.[17]

By building and maintaining such a court, the absolute ruler insured himself against serious attempts by the feudal element to regain its corporate rights of rule.[18] At the same time he compensated it somewhat for the loss by exalting it over the outlying society and holding out to individual courtiers the chance of preferment or the hope of securing a pension or a sinecure. Also, by surrounding himself with the nobility at court, the ruler reasserted the fact that he still shared, as their *primus inter pares*, their distinctive cultural, status, and economic position—though not, of course, their political one.

The ruler, then, ruled *from* his court rather than *through* it. The court made up the expressive aspect of his rule, as it were, but this had to be complemented by an instrumental aspect. Hence intersecting with the court (rather than entirely nested within it) there was another setting, which was placed in a more direct and material relation to the business of rule and which operated as the medium of the ruler's personal power (at least in the case of Louis XIV). This setting involved a few councils of government, each having a small number of members, but each connected with a large number of agents and executors through links all ultimately instituted and activated by the ruler's personal command. As Louis XIV used them, the councils assisted the ruler in the formation of *his* decisions and were responsible to him for carrying them out. Members were personally appointed by the sovereign and operated as his servants, though often they were of noble origin. Those discretionary powers the ruler's servants necessarily had to exercise in order to keep the business of administration going and relieve the ruler of day-to-day decisions were at this stage assigned to them at the ruler's own command, not determined and disciplined by law.[19]

This system of overlapping councils culminated in a small number of ministers bearing various titles—not in *one* minister who by "representing" the system to the ruler might mediate the ruler's control over it. At its base, the system ramified out to include a multitude of lowlier agents—from the officers of the standing army and navy, to those arranging and supervising public works, to the intendants assigned to oversee all governmental and administrative business in a given locality. The roles of all these agents, however different their titles and competences, were patterned after that of the *commissarius*. This was an office of military origin, whose characteristics Hintze defines as follows in order to stress its difference from ständisch, patrimonial offices: "Without a vested right in his post; without ties to the local forces of resistance; untrammeled by superannuated conceptions of right and of time-hallowed official conduct; just an instrument of the higher will, of the new idea of state; unreservedly committed to the prince, empowered by him and dependent on him; no longer an *officier* but a *fonctionnaire*— the Commissarius represents a new type of servant of the state, in accord with the spirit of the absolutist reason of state."[20] Most of the people manning these lower posts were of bourgeois or petty-noble origins, and many were university-trained lawyers. They were committed to performing their function in such a way as to "compensate" for a lowly birth and/or to increase an inadequate family patrimony. Normally, this activated them to great zeal, and often to intense animosity toward those who held traditional, ständisch, or feudal jurisdictional prerogatives whether because they were members of estate bodies or because they or their ascendants had bought offices from the crown.

New Aspects of Rule

Both components of the transition to absolutism considered so far—the Stände's declining capacity for initiative and resistance, and the ruler's offensive—must be related to needs and opportunities for political action arising from the changing societal environment and respectively weakening the Stände's and increasing the ruler's leverage. I have in mind, first, the necessity for new forms of political action whose very novelty "cut off" the Estates. For instance, the new military requirements of European power politics (increasingly focused on the conquest and exploitation of overseas lands), besides decreasing the significance of the traditional leadership skills of the feudal element, made it necessary to gain access to new sources of wealth that traditional levies and tributes could not adequately tap. And we have already seen how

71

by introducing the urban excises the Prussian ruler established a new tax base for his military and administrative apparatus and excluded it from the Estates' control. I also have in mind the demand for uniform, territory-wide regulation of various matters. For instance, between 1665 and 1690 Louis XIV promulgated ordinances and codes that uniformly regulated over all of France such diverse matters as civil and criminal court procedure, the management of forests and rivers, shipping and sailing, and the trade in black slaves. Also in Prussia an enormous body of territory-wide legal rules was produced in the ruler's name, in the guise of police bylaws. It would have been impossible, in both cases, to perform such enterprises through "dualistically" negotiated, ständisch rule-making.

But note that the ruler's enactment of such legislation affected not just the specific interests and activities concerned but the very meaning of law. In the Ständestaat, "the law" was essentially the distinctive packages of rights and privileges traditionally claimed by the estates and their component bodies as well as by the ruler; it existed in the form of differentiated legal entitlements, generally of ancient origin, and it was in principle within the corporate powers of the beneficiaries of those entitlements to uphold them—forcibly, if necessary. Such law could be modified by the Stände when entering into or renewing compacts with the ruler, or by shared deliberations and mutual adjustments between Stände and ruler or between individual Stände. But in principle it could not be modified at the will of any one party, since it was not seen as the product of unilateral will in the first place. As we have noted, the rights and obligations of this or that individual or body were the typical issue of the Ständestaat's political process. But that process as a whole treated the law as a framework, as a set of givens, however contested in its precise significance. The law's validity was seen as resting ultimately on the superhuman agency of the Deity, operating through the slow sedimentation of custom and the negotiated understandings of the legitimate holders of faculties of rule.[21]

Against this background, the idea that the ruler could, by an act of his sovereign will, produce new law and have it enforced by his own increasingly pervasive and effective system of courts was wholly revolutionary. It transformed law from a *framework of* into an *instrument for* rule. Furthermore, since such law was designed to apply uniformly over the territory, the provincial and regional Stände lost the ability to adapt it to local conditions. Through such new law, the ruler addressed himself ever more clearly and compellingly to the whole population of the territory. He disciplined relations in increasingly general and abstract terms, applicable "wherever and whenever." In expressing as law his sovereign will, the ruler contemplated the Estates as (at best) a privileged audience whose individual components might be graciously exempted from the unpleasant effects (especially fiscal ones) of the new rules. But the Stände were no longer capable of seriously modifying or mediating his will, of screening the larger society from it.

This new approach to law and its relations to rule appears even more significant in the light of two facts. First, paralleling the growth of legislation enacted by the ruler and enforced by his courts was the vast phenomenon of the "reception of Roman law," whereby the legal principles and rules of Justinian's *Corpus juris civilis* acquired validity over several territories.[22] Though not entirely coincident with the rise of absolutism either geographically or chronologically, this development was very much in the spirit of the absolutist system of rule[23] (and was consonant with the advance of commercialization and individualism in the socioeconomic and cultural spheres). With the "reception," an enormous range of diverse social relations came to be legally regulated in ways that often differed widely from those of the "good old law," often of Germanic-feudal origin, that had sometimes been elaborated and modified by urban corporations.[24] Second, though the rulers increasingly posited themselves as the founts of law, whether directly or indirectly by reference to Roman law, they did not consider themselves bound by it. It is one of the original meanings of the very notion of "absolutism" that the ruler himself is *legibus solutus*: the law, being a product of his sovereign power, cannot bind him or set boundaries to that power.

The ruler now possesses in the law a flexible, indefinitely extensible and modifiable instrument for articulating and sanctioning his will. As a result, his power ceases to be conceived as a collection of discrete rights and prerogatives, as it had been under the Ständestaat, and becomes instead more unitary and abstract, more *potential*, as it were. As such, it begins to detach itself conceptually from the physical person of the ruler; we might put it another way and say that it subsumes the ruler within itself, radiating *its own* energy through him. This is part of the significance of Louis XIV's court, where though the figure of the king was exalted to superhuman proportions, diffusing a light of unearthly intensity ("le Roi soleil"), it stood for a project, an entity, a power much greater than the king himself.

The Ruler and His Bureaucracy: Prussia

In the eighteenth-century phase of the absolutist system of rule, best represented by Prussia under Frederick William I (1713–40) and Frederick the Great (1740–86), the court lost much of the political significance it possessed in the France of Louis XIV. In Prussia the function of projecting the superiority of the state's power over the "physical king" himself shifted to the military and administrative apparatus. Louis XIV had ruled, as I said, *from* a lofty, resplendent court of which he was the pinnacle, with the assistance of a few small councils of personal advisers and ministers. Frederick William I and his successor ruled through, at the center of, a much larger, more elaborately constructed and regulated body of public organs engaged in administrative activities that were more continuous, systematic, pervasive, visible, and effective than anything Louis XIV had ever contemplated.

An essential component of this development was a new body of law—"public law"—specifically concerned with the construction and operation of the administrative system.[25] The system's members operated not immediately on a commission from the ruler, nor as the direct executors of his personal commands, but rather under the guidance and control of a body of enacted norms that articulated the state's power (unitarily conceived) into a number of functions each of which was entrusted to an organ, i.e., a set of coordinated offices empowered to form and enforce authoritative decisions. Each organ possessed precisely delimited competences, standards by which to evaluate their exercise, and formal and material faculties for operation.

The individuals manning such organs were functionaries (*Beamte*) duly appointed to the component offices of each organ and supposedly trained and tested in the business of those offices. They possessed no proprietary rights in their posts and could make no claim to any revenues that might accrue from their work, being remunerated instead according to a fixed scale from central funds. The law regulated the higher powers of command, supervision, and discipline to which the functionaries were subject. Except at the highest level, where peculiarly "political" decisions were taken on matters concerning the internal and external security of the state or the broader directions of its policy, all individual decisions were to be reached through juristic reasoning—applying general legal provisions to carefully ascertained and documented circumstances. Moreover, all such business was transacted in writing and recorded in files.

Thus the state was intended to operate as the instrument of its own enacted laws, thereby making its activities systematized, coordinated, predictable, machinelike, and impersonal. The principle that the law is not binding on the sovereign power that produces it, however, was preserved. "Public law," then, was a set of arrangements internal to the system, and as such regulated the operation of lower offices vis-à-vis higher ones; but it vested no actionable claims in individual subjects in their private capacities. A semijudicial system for monitoring the impact of the administration's activities on rightful private interests might be maintained, but again it would be largely an internal arrangement that would not empower private individuals as outsiders to block or frustrate administrative decisions.

In essence, then, in the "Prussian model" the state was made transcendent over the physical person of its head through the depersonalization and objectification of its power. Public law shaped the state as an artificial, organizational entity operating through individuals who in principle were interchangeable and who in their official activities were expected to employ their certified abilities in stewardlike loyalty to the state and commitment to its interests. Schiera summarizes the administration-building process culminating under Frederick the Great as follows:

The prince managed to replace the ständisch administrative system with one of his own, based on functionaries who depended directly on him, were faithful to him, and occupied offices of commissarial origin. Although bound to the prince personally, at the same time the functionaries made up a unified entity, endowed with a dynamic internal to it, that did not rest entirely upon the prince's own person. It was always the prince who coordinated the activities of the various branches of the administration; but the latter operated under its own steam, thanks to its own organizational structure. There was a bond between the administration and the prince, and a tight bond indeed; but its effects were filtered, as it were, through the now central concept of "salus publica," or the common good. Formally the relationship to the prince was still a personal one, but the person itself of the prince had begun to matter largely to the extent that he himself was considered as the first servant of the state.[26]

Whereas Louis XIV had ruled surrounded by court nobles engaged in status display (and in displaying their status they exalted his), Frederick the Great ruled as the first among a vast number of officials. Many of these were nobles, but once again they only maintained their privileged position by accepting new terms—the ruler's. In both France and Prussia the resistance of the Stände was so thoroughly diminished under absolutism that the political process could no longer be said to revolve around the allocation of faculties of rule within the state. All significant faculties were gathered into the hands of the ruler, and the prime political issues became how to increase (in absolute rather than in relative terms) the ruler's power and how to use that increased power internally and externally.

Between the end of the eighteenth and the beginning of the nineteenth century, both issues found significantly new resolution in a novel type of rule system that on the one hand continued the main trends in the state's constitution and organization already evident under absolutism (though in a modified and selective manner), but on the other hand changed (much more considerably) the relations between the state and the larger society. The tendencies and contrasts inherent in those relations under absolutism must now be briefly pointed out.

The Emergence of the Civil Society

As we have seen, the absolutist ruler had gathered unto himself those faculties of rule that under the Ständestaat were dispersed among several privileged individuals and bodies. He had concentrated those faculties, together with those of ancient, regalian origins, into a unitary apparatus for the formation and execution of statewide policies, organized as an increasingly effective machine for exercising alone all aspects of rule, and operating in the name and in the interests of sovereignty.

We have also seen that, as a consequence, the privileged individuals and bodies had become, more and more exclusively, the holders of legally favored private capacities, the privileged pursuers of private interests. But in the past, the Stände's political prerogatives had been the glue that held together their components—Stand with Stand, household with household within each Stand. Thus, as those political prerogatives were effectively confiscated by the ruler, the Stände began to "come unstuck."[27]

On the other hand, the state's institutions (first particularly the court, later the ministerial and administrative system) had become increasingly *public*: that is, official, highly distinctive, relatively visible. The state's codes and statutes, of course, had to be officially promulgated and published, printed in the vulgar tongue, widely

77

diffused. In various countries the adoption of uniforms for both military and civilian functionaries of the state placed the same emphasis on the distinctiveness and unity of the state apparatus.

Thus the state had moved, as it were, up and away from the larger society to a level of its own, where specifically political personnel and functions were concentrated. At the same time, the state was empowered to affect with its action the whole society. That society, from the height of the state's level, appeared to be peopled exclusively by a multitude of *particuliers*, of private (though sometimes privileged) individuals. The state addressed them in their capacity as subjects, taxpayers, potential military draftees, etc.; but it considered them unqualified to take an active part in its own business. It contemplated the civil society exclusively as a suitable object of rule.

And indeed, a prime concern of absolutist rule was exactly the authoritative regulation and promotion of the private preoccupations of individuals—primarily the economic ones. In the seventeenth century, as we have seen, this concern led the state to endorse, make uniform, and modify as needed the rules that over the previous few centuries guilds and other urban corporate bodies had autonomously and locally imposed upon commercial and productive pursuits: rules setting prices and standards for merchandise, specifying productive processes, regulating the training of apprentices, controlling competition and innovation. Other aspects of mercantilism—and particularly the concern with the positive balance of trade and the building up of a country's bullion reserves —suggest that perhaps it should not be seen as exclusively or even primarily concerned with promoting the country's (or the bourgeoisie's) economic well-being. Rather, economic activity was promoted (1) to keep the population busy, peaceful, and unconcerned with political business, and (2) to generate the taxable wealth needed to underwrite both the wasteful aspects of the system of rule (foremost, its often disastrously expensive court) and its increasingly costly international ventures.

In the eighteenth century, this latter objective of absolutist policy was even more persistently and commandingly in view than in the seventeenth. By this time, however, mercantilist policies proper had been largely abandoned in favor of those that made up the economic policy of so-called "enlightened despotism."[28] These latter policies, however, revealed and often unwittingly fostered the start of a remarkable change in the internal configuration and political significance of civil society. In the long run, such change would transform the system of rule by realizing the civil society's demand for an active, decisive role in the political process. Let us turn now to the matter of identifying the social groups whose distinctive "ideal and material interests" led them to articulate that demand.

The Civil Society's Political Challenge

During the historical career of absolutism, an increasingly significant section of the European bourgeoisie—the capitalist entrepreneurs—had been redefining their social identity as that of a *class*, no longer as that of an *estate*. This phenomenon, an intrinsic aspect of the advance of the capitalist mode of production, had been occasionally favored and accelerated by public policies. Since it was to have decisive political consequences, let us briefly characterize it here.

A class is a collective unit more abstract, more impersonal, more distinctively translocal than an estate. Its visible boundaries are set not by a style of life or a specific mode of activity, but by the possession of or exclusion from market resources that give their possessors a claim to the appropriation of a disproportionate share of the social product, and that as a consequence can be accumulated and continuously redeployed on the market. In the case of the groups we are considering, the resource in question is capital, privately owned.

The unity of a class, unlike that of an estate, is not maintained by internal organs of authority that guard the traditional rights, particular and common, of the collectivity and enforce discipline on its individual components. A class presupposes and admits competition for advantage among its components, who are all private, self-interested individuals. However, such competition is supposed to be self-equilibrating; it thus limits and legitimizes a given component's advantage over others. Moreover, competition within a class is limited by the recognition of certain shared interests among all components in the face of antagonist classes on the market.

Thus the political needs of a class possessing critical market resources are different from those of an estate. Such a class does not require that it be directly vested with powers of rule, since the exercise of rule from within the class would arbitrarily (and thus illegitimately) advantage some competitors against others and would interfere both with the market's supposed capacity for self-equilibration and with the process of accumulation. On the other hand, such a class cannot dispense with rule altogether: it needs some agency to exercise rule both to safeguard the autonomous workings of the market and to guarantee the class's collective appropriation of its distinctive resources (and their apportionment to individuals' private control) against any attack on the part of an antagonist class; it also needs that agency to exercise rule from a unitary center structurally apart from and above all classes in a distinctive, "public," sovereign sphere of its own.

Now the absolutist system constituted exactly such a distinctive, "public," sovereign concentration of faculties of rule, and hence it constituted a fitting political environment for the transformation into a class of a part of the bourgeoisie. However, the absolutist emphases on purposeful intervention in business matters, on monopolies, on restraints on competition, and on direction of trade interfered with the autonomy and the fluidity of the market—and the market is where a class both moderates its internal contrasts through competition and maintains its collective advantage by accumulating and utilizing the resources it has appropriated.[29*]

It is commonly argued that the interest of the bourgeoisie-as-class in the autonomy of the market led it to pose a radical political challenge to absolutism. Yet such a notion is surely too simplistic. One might argue that whatever the negative effects of absolutist "interference with the market" on the interests of the class in question, they were probably amply compensated by internal and external policies favoring accumulation and preserving private control over most of a nation's capital. Besides, the bourgeois political demands vulgarly summarized as "laissez-faire, laissez-passer" were in fact raised not so much *against* as *toward* the absolutist system, which in its later phase did its best to accommodate them. Such demands could be amply met while keeping the whole civil society, including its economically ascendant class, as a "suitable object of rule" (as we phrased it above). As late as the close of the nineteenth century, the case of Germany shows that a bourgeoisie could draw most of the benefits of capitalist industrialization without aggressively claiming its own political birthright.

We need to assess additional factors to explain why most national bourgeoisies did pose a thoroughgoing challenge to the respective *anciens régimes*. In my view, such bourgeoisies were politically radicalized and "energized" by components of them distinct from the entrepreneurial groups we have considered so far (though sometimes overlapping with them). These components were involved particularly in intellectual, literary, and artistic pursuits, and had been developing a distinct social identity—that of a *public*, or rather, at first, of a variety of "publics." [30] They had been increasingly carrying out their pursuits in distinctive settings and media (from scientific societies, literary salons, Masonic lodges,[31] and coffeehouses to publishing houses and the daily and periodical press) that were public in being accessible to all interested comers, or at least to all those possessing appropriate, objectively ascertainable qualifications, such as learning, technical competence, relevant information, persuasive eloquence, creative imagination, and capacity for critical judgment. Furthermore, all participants were allowed to contribute to the open-ended, relatively unconstrained process of argument intended to produce a widely held, critically established "public opinion" about any given theme.[32]

At an early stage in the development of such publics their

themes had been mainly scientific, literary, and philosophical; their arguments had been mainly confined to such areas as the development of taste, the attainment and dissemination of knowledge about natural phenomena, and the refinements of moral sensibility both in the immediate participants and, through them, in a wider, literate public. When not hindered by censorship and repression, however, topics had progressively shifted toward distinctively political matters: the characteristic civic virtues and vices of "the nation"; the ways and means to the promotion of its welfare; the improvement of legislation; the relations between church and state; the conduct of foreign affairs.

In this way, certain social groups—predominantly bourgeois, though sometimes mixed with elements from the nobility and the lower clergy—progressively put themselves forward as an audience qualified to criticize the state's own operation. They were seeking, as it were, to complement the "public sphere" constructed from above with a "public realm" formed by individual members of the civil society transcending their private concerns, elaborating a "public opinion" on matters of state and bringing it to bear on the activities of state organs.

Now any attempt to institutionalize criticism and controversy, and to assign to both a role in steering the actions of the state, posed to the absolutist system a challenge more direct than the "class" demand that it should respect the market's capacity for self-regulation. A "reasoning public" might lead the civil society to break through the passive, subject position in which the official power sought to confine it. The reasoning public not only dared to open debate on matters that those powers had ever treated as *arcana imperii*, but threatened to extend that debate to wider and wider social circles in order to increase its support.

More threatening than these largely potential challenges, though, was the bourgeois attack on the notion of privilege, of ascribed, particular rights attached to certain ranks. This struck directly at the absolutist policy of compensating the traditional estates for their political losses by maintaining their status advantages and shoring up their economic position. The commitment of large sectors of bourgeois opinion to secular enlightenment—with its aggressive rationalism, its antitraditionalism, and its emphasis on emancipation—threatened that "alliance of the throne and the altar" typical of many absolutist states. Opinion-makers who suggested that *national* interests[33]* and the public welfare should guide foreign and internal policies were an embarrassment to monarchs vestigially attached to dynastic interests and still surrounded by the absurdly wasteful pomp of their courts.

On the other hand, some aspects of the development of "public opinion on public affairs" were compatible with absolutist policies and constituted ideological endorsements of them. The very existence of a public realm was largely the consequence of the absolutist state's policy of bypassing the Stände and addressing directly the generality of its subjects through its laws, its taxation, its uniform and pervasive administration, its increasing appeal to patriotism. Nor did the bourgeois public claim for itself independent, self-standing, self-enforcing powers of rule, as the Stände had done. It recognized the ruler's claims of sovereignty and the distinctiveness of the enterprise of rule. It was quick to endorse his declared commitment to national greatness, to the promotion of the people's welfare. It considered problems high on the ruler's agenda—from legislative reform to the promotion of industry—and brought to bear on them resources of sense, competence, and concern as well as a capacity for informed and critical judgment that it was in the ruler's own interest to mobilize and tap. There was, furthermore, between members of the bourgeois public and the personnel of the ruler's own apparatus an increasing similarity in social background, in moral and intellectual concerns, in learning, and in academic qualifications.

Such convergences of interests and aspirations between the bourgeoisie-as-public and the absolutist state suggest that the former did not necessarily pose an outright challenge to the latter. Neither, I argued above, did the bourgeoisie-as-class. However, the latter was bound to find attractive the prospect of a newly designed system of rule that would institutionalize and place at the very center of the system a new notion of "the public" as a realm open to individual members of the civil society, responsive to their views and interests, and operating through the open-ended confrontation of opinions.

In this new design, the public realm would not just critically monitor the operations of the state but initiate, direct, and control them. Its legitimation to do so would come from its *representation* of opinions prevalent in the civil society, which by the same token would become the *constituency* of the system of rule rather than simply its object. The public realm—once constituted as an elected assembly placed at the very center of the state—would serve that constituency and activate the state on its behalf by framing as general and abstract laws the prevalent orientations of opinion on given issues as reflected in the formation of majorities and minorities among the elected representatives.

Since the bourgeois class was the dominant force within the civil society, representation would reflect that dominance by being weighted in favor of "enlightened" and "responsible" opinions. This would be done through the objective workings of the mechanism of representation, and in particular through the qualifications impartially required of electors and representatives—*not* through the attaching of political prerogatives to individual members of any class, which would deprive them of their essential quality as private individuals.

Because general and abstract, the laws enacted by the assembly would respect and safeguard the market's autonomy and capacity for self-regulation, and at the same time would uphold the market advantages of the capital-owning class—but again without singling them out as politically privileged. Other laws would empower the state organs (again abstractly and generally) to carry out individual acts of rule.

This vision of a new constitutional design of the state, largely projecting the distinctive claims and aspirations of the bourgeoisie-as-public, was what in my view "energized" politically the bourgeoisie-as-class and generated the increasing tension between both sectors of the bourgeoisie and the late-absolutist *ancien régime*. The historical developments through which this tension was resolved—mainly through the realization of the above design—are too varied and complex to be reviewed here. Nonetheless, two dimensions of those developments deserve mention: first, the importance of ideas of nationality and national sovereignty; and second, the extent to which the emerging proletariat, despite its inherent antagonism to the bourgeois class, found itself fighting on behalf of the bourgeois political design.

In many Western countries the progress of the new system of rule was marked by political revolutions; but this should not lead us to overestimate the "break" between the absolutist system and the one that followed it (the subject of the next chapter). As Tocqueville established in his study of the greatest of those revolutions, there were numerous and significant elements of continuity between pre- and postrevolutionary political systems.

There were two principal reasons for such continuity, one external and the other internal. On the one hand, the significance of power relations between states not only persisted but was enhanced by ideas of nationality and by the European "scramble" for the markets and resources of other parts of the world. On the other, there was the growing complexity of the civil society itself, and the increasing intensity of its class conflicts. On both counts, it was in the interest of the bourgeois class to maintain and even to strengthen the state's potential for societal guidance, for the defense of national boundaries, and for the moderation or repression of conflict—aspects of rule that over the centuries had become built into the state apparatus. That apparatus had to be made amenable to control by the institutionalized public realm, not dismantled, weakened, or seriously damaged in its ability to exercise rule over society. For the same reasons, the bourgeoisie, in putting forward and realizing its political program, had to guard against the potential democratic-populist implications of such ideas as popular sovereignty or equality of citizenship.

CHAPTER V

The Nineteenth-Century Constitutional State

OUR ARGUMENT thus far has drawn most of its conceptual guidance and empirical support from the writings of historians of political institutions. In this chapter I shall rely instead mainly on literature from the field of constitutional law. Although these two traditions of scholarship—the historical and the juridical —sometimes overlap, the reader may feel a shift of emphasis, which I shall justify as follows.

I have already suggested that through the whole course of development of the modern state legal argument, the appeal to notions of justice and the rightfulness of one's claim, constituted a distinctive and significant (through seldom decisive) component of the political process. In the feudal and the ständisch systems of rule, such argument mainly took the form of the assertion of and confrontation over differentiated *rights*; that is, each party put forward particular tradition-based claims to specific prerogatives and immunities. Argument of this type did not easily lend itself to the highly abstract and formal mode of juristic speech that became possible when the law began to be seen as primarily constituted not of differentiated claims but of general and abstract commands, whose validity stemmed simply from the expressed will of the sovereign, and whose effect was to form a unitary, logically homogeneous and coherent, and gapless system of rules.[1]

This latter conception of law—already entailed in the "reception" of Roman law, in absolutist codifications, and in bureaucratic "public law"—triumphed in the late eighteenth and nineteenth centuries. On the basis of this notion of law, the Continental universities developed a new body of juristic thinking that had constitutional and administrative law as its main components and the state as its main referent. In its best products, this form of juristic thinking constitutes a new, sophisticated kind of "speech about rule" characterized by an urge toward systematization of its subject matter and by a penchant for sustained conceptual analysis.

In the hands of some practitioners, this approach to the study of rule often attains levels of sophisticated abstraction that make it at best irrelevant to our concerns here, and at worst positively misleading and mystifying. In my judgment, however, these excesses do not make the approach less deserving of selective and critical attention within a sociological treatment. Accordingly this chapter, which sketches the broad institutional features of the nineteenth-century constitutional state (some of which were already evident under earlier rule systems), will draw freely on formulations offered by constitutional lawyers and occasionally point up sociologically relevant considerations they tend to ignore. More such considerations will be introduced in the following chapter, which raises the question of the relationship between state and society.

The argument will be at a high level of abstraction throughout, ignoring considerable differences in the constitutional structures of, say, nineteenth-century Britain and late-nineteenth-century Germany in order to highlight the features they had in common with each other and with most other Western states.

Sovereignty and the States System

Let us begin by noting some important aspects of the states system as it had evolved by the nineteenth century. Every state exists, first of all, in the presence of and in competition with other states like it. Together, these states make up a system fundamentally different from an ancient empire, with its heterocephalic, semi-sovereign components tied to an imperial center by relations of subordination. The modern states system is made up of coordinate, juxtaposed, sovereign units. Individual states are not the *organs* of the states system, for they are not posited and empowered by it; states do not derive their faculties of rule from the states system, but possess them rather under equal, self-standing title. The states do not *presuppose* the system, they *generate* it. What orderliness exists in the relations among such units results not from shared submission to an overarching power but from concurrent, voluntary observance of certain rules of mutual conduct in each state's pursuit of its own interests. If one means by "order" the existence of uniformities of conduct generated by compliance with binding norms established through commands and legitimately enforced by an overriding fount and center of order, then no order can be said to exist within this states system. For here the political universe is intrinsically and irremediably "open at the top"—highly contingent, inherently dangerous.[2]

Within the states system, then, each state is a self-originating, self-empowered unit operating exclusively in pursuit of its own interests. But each state's definition of its interests is continuously being modified in response to changes in the internal and external demographic, military, economic, and political environment; and this in turn means that the equilibrium of the system is precarious and continuously in need of readjustment, which, as I indicated, cannot be brought about by the operation of binding norms, since strictly speaking no such norms exist between states. This configuration of relations among major political entities—which, as we saw in Chapter 1, is central to Carl Schmitt's conception of politics —is historically unique to the post-Medieval West. Previously, each high-culture area had been dominated by an empire that considered itself essentially alone in the world as it knew it, and that treated each major political entity within its own area as subordinate to itself.[3] As one writer put it, "at the height of its greatness the Roman empire shared the world with three others just as powerful, and arguably as important: the Han, the Kushan, and the Parthian."[4]

In the post-Classical West, both the Christian Church and the Holy Roman Empire had tried, jointly or separately, to operate as the center of such a hierarchical, imperial framework. But because or in spite of their extensive similarities and mutual dependence, they achieved a deadlock that was among the causes of the emergence of a novel, and drastically different, pattern of relations among increasingly autonomous states.[5] This pattern was consecrated by the Peace of Westphalia (1648), the cornerstone of the modern system of international relations. In the words of Leo Gross, the Peace resulted in

a new system characterized by the coexistence of a multiplicity of states, each sovereign within its own territory, equal to one another, and free from any external earthly authority. The idea of an authority or organization above the sovereign states is no longer. . . . This new system rests on international law and the balance of power—a law operating between rather than above states, and a power operating between rather than above states. . . . The idea of an international community becomes almost an empty phrase, and international law comes to depend upon the will of states concerned with the preservation and expansion of their power.[6]

The extension of this system beyond its original European heartland to the entire planet in our times has been a deeply contradictory process. On the one hand, it has made the world politically a single *oikoumene*;[7] on the other, it has fragmented it into many, often fissiparous states, each claiming ultimate sovereign rule over a segment of the globe. In the nineteenth century, however, this process was far from completion. Through various colonial and "imperial" arrangements (and note the largely novel meaning of the term "imperial"), the "comity of nations" was spreading into lands distant from its heartland; but it was not yet coterminous with the globe and was economically, culturally, and ideologically less heterogeneous than it was to become in the following century. Within this context, the abstract and essentially fictional notion of the equality of all states as sovereign possessed considerable credibility. After all, as Cavour and Bismarck proved, even weaker and peripheral states could dramatically increase their strength and standing through shrewd and bold diplomatic and military action. The states system was intrinsically dynamic because of the persistent tension between, on the one hand, the absoluteness of the notions of sovereignty and *raison d'état* (which articulated and legitimated each state's commitment to self-aggrandizement), and, on the other, the continuous and inescapable presence of other states bounding that "will to sovereignty." Over and over again, each state came up against *limits* to its sovereignty in the form of competing states striving to satisfy their own self-defined interests. Hence in this system every accommodation was conditional, every alliance temporary, and every claim ultimately enforceable only through coercion—if necessary on the field of battle. Under increasingly thick layers of speculative justification and juristic elaboration, the notion of sovereignty in essence came down to purely matter-of-fact realities, as international law acknowledged in the "effectiveness principle": that is, the limits to a state's sovereignty were seen to be the limits to its ability to make good a particular claim. For instance, it was of no use for a state to claim sovereignty over territory that it could not effectively police, and that it could not keep from being policed by other states.[8]

"Might makes right" is less a shockingly crude than a strikingly succinct formulation of such a state of affairs. The inherent instability of the states system was heightened by the growing elaboration in nineteenth-century Europe of two often contradictory criteria by which claims to sovereignty could be made (whether to international law agencies, potential allies, or "world opinion"). One was the principle of "nationality," by which a state would claim that populations currently subject to a neighboring state were "nationally" the same as the claimant's own population and hence should join the latter in a single system of rule. The other was the cry for "natural borders," physical boundaries that would provide the state with military defensibility and a sense of integrity and completeness. Both notions could be advanced or rejected as seemed suitable under particular conditions, and it was not unusual for a state in one instance to make demands on the basis of "nationality" while rejecting a contending state's appeal to "natural borders," and in another (and perhaps contemporaneous) instance do just the reverse—use "natural borders" as the basis for a demand against arguments of "nationality."[9]

In the course of the nineteenth century, hundreds of territorial disputes, diplomatic incidents, colonial clashes, and regional or otherwise limited armed conflicts testified to the tensions built into the structure of the states system. It was thus a considerable achievement, and one needing some explanation, that before 1914 the Western nations knew a "hundred years peace"[10]—that is, the absence of a general European or worldwide war. Here only a few aspects of such an explanation can be suggested. First, hostility between members of the European "comity of nations" found expression mainly in other parts of the world, which were being colonized or otherwise exploited. Second, the experience of the Revolutionary and Napoleonic wars of 1792–1815 had demonstrated both the disastrously bloody and expensive nature of sustained, large-scale modern warfare and the threatening connection between war and social revolution. Third, it was the interests of the national bourgeoisies that increasingly determined the policies of states in the nineteenth century and oriented states in the first place to the promotion of industry, trade, and colonial expansion rather than war. Finally, sophisticated diplomatic and semijudicial arrangements had been constructed since the Peace of Westphalia for avoiding, moderating, and settling interstate conflicts.

Yet the enormity of the breakdown of the states system in 1914 bespeaks the magnitude, multiplicity, and asperity of the tensions it had generated and allowed to accumulate. In particular, the competition among national sections of the Western bourgeoisie over the resources of nonstate, semistate, or pseudostate areas of the world had ceased to constitute a safety valve for the states system and had indeed become the fount of its most acute tensions and imbalances.[11]

In summary, the sovereignty of the Western states, originally won at the expense of the Empire and the Papacy, became progressively established until in the nineteenth century those states did not so much live in as themselves make up an intrinsically open-ended, risk-filled, and tension-fraught world. Various devices imparted some ordering to that world: the conduct of continuous, highly professionalized, largely secret diplomacy; the purposeful unleashing of "opinion campaigns" by one state to bring pressure on another; the institutionalized provision of third-party mediation and arbitration; and finally, the threat or waging of war. Each state was committed to the use of these and other devices in defense of its sovereignty, for no state could long survive unless it was prepared to back up whatever rights it claimed to possess.

The Unity of the State

We have looked thus far at some implications of sovereignty external to a given system of rule, that is, affecting one state's relations to others. But it is a feature of the nineteenth-century state that each operates in its own territory as the sole, exclusive fount of all powers and prerogatives of rule. This attainment of unitary internal sovereignty (in some places achieved under absolutism), after centuries of development in this direction, is an outstanding characteristic of the constitutional state of the nineteenth century. To employ David Easton's terminology, all social activities directly involving the "authoritative allocation of value" at the societal level are carried out by a single decision center—the state itself—no matter how internally differentiated and extensively ramified those activities might be. No individual or corporate body can engage in activities of rule except as an organ, agent, or delegate of the state; and the state alone assigns and determines the extent of those activities according to its own rules, backed by its own sanctions. States may be very differently constituted internally—they may or may not, for instance, envisage the citizenry as their ultimate constituency and the seat of sovereignty; they may make the head of state into a chief executive or into a figurehead—but regardless of variations, no nineteenth-century state is constituted and operates "dualistically," in Gierke's sense of the term, as the Ständestaat was and did with its characteristic counterposing of *rex et regnum*, each holding distinctive, independent powers of rule. Mature modern states are intrinsically "monistic," and represent in this a return to the Roman tradition, whereby the *princeps*'s power was derived from the will of the *populus*.[12] The Continental juristic construction of the state as a person is a characteristically sophisticated way of expressing this principle.

Let us look at other, more matter-of-fact expressions of it, all to a greater or lesser extent characteristic of the nineteenth-century state. There is unity of the state's territory, which comes to be bounded as much as possible by a continuous geographical frontier that is militarily defensible. There is a single currency and a unified fiscal system. Generally, there is a single "national" language. (This is often artificially superimposed upon a variety of local languages and dialects, which sometimes are harshly suppressed but more often are slowly uprooted by an expanding public-education system employing the national language. Moreover, the creation of a literary tradition in the national language works to erode cultural particularism.) Finally, there is a unified legal system that allows alternative juridical traditions to maintain validity only in peripheral areas and for limited purposes.

Some Western states had been achieving these goals progressively during the course of a few centuries. In the nineteenth century, all states pursued them self-consciously and explicitly, often in connection with ideas of nationality. Of course this drive toward unity met resistance, which was sometimes successful: the most significant exceptions to the principle of unity were federal states; but even there the principle was embodied in a federal constitution and a federal government charged (at the very least) with the conduct of foreign relations. Otherwise, resistance at best slowed down the drive for unity. Local recruitment of ancient military units, for instance, gave way to a system of conscription that shuffled recruits around the state's territory in such a way that they found themselves stationed in localities they often did not feel were part of their country.[13*] Dialects and minority languages gave way before the growing public-education systems, which celebrated the virtues and achievements of dynasts and statesmen who were often not merely unknown but literally foreign to the pupils. Local worthies and notables who sought to preserve their standing in the community as men of judgment and influence had to learn new and baffling political games, had to explore novel avenues of access to different centers of power, had to operate according to unfamiliar rules.

More significant than the resistances and adaptations to the unifying drive of the nineteenth-century states are perhaps two contradictions within it. First, despite sophisticated legal mechanisms of delegation, appointment, and accountability employed to connect the power center of the unitary state with its increasingly ramified administrative apparatus and to make its organs responsive to central instructions, powerful countertendencies are at work within the system making sections of it increasingly autonomous. Different ministries within the same central government, for instance, possess or develop distinctive administrative styles, clienteles, policy traditions, and biases in the selection and training of their personnel. Thus rivalries and policy differences develop among them and make coordination difficult. The army, the police, the diplomatic service, and sometimes top judicial bodies maintain substantially autonomous lines and traditions of political action, with the result that each operates in some cases as a "state within the state," as a de facto holder of autonomous political prerogatives.

Second, the nature of capitalism as a system of power between classes also affects, in less visible though no less substantial ways, the notion of the unity of the state's power. Particularly in the Jacobin tradition, that notion entailed that in the modern state "vertical," power-focused, and power-activated relations could obtain only between the state itself and private individuals; among the latter, all relations were supposed to be "horizontal," contractual, and power-free. But the possession of capital is a *legally and politically protected means* to the creation and reproduction of de facto relations of domination between individuals belonging to different classes. The contradiction is apparent: a state that purports to be the source of all power relations acts in fact as the guarantor of power relations that do not originate from itself, and that it does not control—those engendered by the institution of private control over capital.[14]

The "Modernity" of the State

For all its structural complexity and the vastness and continuity of its operations, the modern state—like any other institutional complex—resolves ultimately into social processes patterned by certain rules. One may thus gain some conceptual purchase on the nature of the modern state—as against that of other large-scale systems of rule—by inquiring into what is distinctive about its patterns. The institutional profile of the modern state obtained in this way emphasizes, by and large, its "modernity," since its patterns appear to be the products of an advanced and sophisticated process of social differentiation.

To begin with, the modern state appears as an artificial, engineered institutional complex rather than as one that has developed spontaneously by accretion. It is a deliberately erected framework. As the previous chapters have suggested, the development of particular states—however protracted, and however different in tempos, sequences, and concrete stages from place to place—on the whole bears out well our contemporary image of state-*building*, with its connotations of purposive effort and conscious arrangement to a design. Conceptually speaking, the state of the late-eighteenth and nineteenth centuries, in particular, often owes its existence to an act of (collective) will and deliberation, sometimes embodied in explicit constitutional enactments. But even over the previous centuries, the formation of various Western states appears imputable to something German scholars—even the less fanciful-minded, like Hermann Heller—are fond of calling *Wille zum Staat*, the will to put a state into being.[15] In other words, the modern state is not bestowed upon a people as a gift by God, its own *Geist*, or blind historical forces; it is a "made" reality.

Once "made," moreover, a state constantly operates with reference to some idea of an end or function to which it is instrumental. It is not a contrivance only in the sense that purposive action lies behind it, as it were, in the process of its emergence; ahead of it, too, lies a distinctive though complex task that constitutes the justification for its existence and the reason for its operations. Now this imputation of a teleological basis to the state is controversial, if only because if used to *define* the state, it would follow that a state ceases to be one to the extent that it does not in fact direct its activity to its particular goal. Thus it is often suggested that the definition of a "modern state" should refer not to any finite set of ends the state might possess but only to its structural features (among which the most distinctive has often been seen to be the monopoly of legitimate violence).[16] Alternatively, it is sometimes suggested that the state in fact does by its very nature possess a *telos*, but that this is wholly internal to the state itself, consisting exclusively of the continuous expansion of its own power.

However, we are seeking here not to define the state, but simply to characterize the institutional patterns governing its operations; in this respect, it seems plausible to agree with Heller that the "function" of the state is "the autonomous organization and activation of the social process over the state's territory, grounded in the historical need that some modus vivendi be achieved among the contrasting interests operating in a given section of the globe."[17] Note that this statement leaves open the question of which among the "contrasting interests" are, or may be, systematically favored by the "modus vivendi" the state upholds.

A further characteristic of the state, closely connected with its "engineered" and teleological nature, is its "functional specificity": that is, the state does not claim or attempt to encompass and control the totality of social existence. The latter is contemplated (and served, according to the functional argument above) from a specific viewpoint, with reference to some discrete, abstract, differentiated aspects of it. The state presupposes and complements a manifold social reality (encompassing, for instance, the social standing, religious affiliations, and economic resources of individuals) that under previous arrangements directly and immediately affected and was affected by the activities of rule; now, however, a set of filters of significance, of standards of mediation, of codings and decodings blocks off such direct mutual effects.[18]

No longer, as with the Greek *politeia*, is the state directly identified with the society at large. The citizens' commitment to the welfare and security of the state is no longer activated by personal loyalty to a chief. Posts carrying specific political responsibilities and faculties are no longer assigned directly on grounds of wealth, rank, or religious standing. The state's increasingly vast and expensive operations are financed from a distinctively public store of wealth, one that is replenished by levying taxes impersonally on the citizens' incomes and expenditure—not by extorting donations from them, selling them offices or shares in the proceeds of the state's military or colonial ventures, or drawing on their private wealth.[19] The state, as we shall see below, lays down frameworks for the pursuit by its citizens of the most diverse private interests.[20] Its demands on individuals may be heavy (often extending to military service in murderous wars); but again it addresses individuals in their differentiated, abstract capacity as citizens.

As this last point suggests, there is a distinctively universalistic tone to the typical relation of the state to its citizenry. Citizenship itself is acquired chiefly by virtue of an individual's birth within the state's territory; it is in principle an equal, nonparticularistic capacity. The laws, which as we shall see are the language in which the state chiefly addresses citizens, are typically *general* commands taking no account of individual conditions other than those they themselves abstractly constitute as relevant.

Finally, the state is internally structured as a formal, complex organization. It is composed of organs—that is, of interdependent, never wholly autonomous loci for deciding, controlling, and executing policy—whose spheres of competence, whose resources, and whose modalities of operation are determined from outside by other, superordinate organs (until one is attained that carries ulti-

97

mate authority). Each organ is in turn constituted as a set of differentiated and complementary offices, mostly hierarchically arranged. The occupancy of these offices is regulated by universalistic criteria that in turn assign the occupant nonappropriated, impersonal, "public" powers and responsibilities. The competition for and exercise of political power within a society constituted as a modern state typically involve the seeking and manning of "offices" and the exercise of influence on their operation. (Note that "influence" can hardly, by its very nature, be distributed and brought to bear according to universalistic terms.) Offices normally operate by referring to publicly sanctioned decision criteria and standards of execution, not by relying on ad hoc justifications.

In sum, the state is designed, and is intended to operate, as a machine whose parts all mesh, a machine propelled by energy and directed by information flowing from a single center in the service of a plurality of coordinated tasks. This machine imagery is more plausible when applied to the state's administrative apparatus than when applied to other parts of the system of rule. Yet the time-worn image of "checks and balances" applied to the division of powers among all higher constitutional organs is quite as mechanical. The state is not *just* a contrivance: it is a complex and sophisticated contrivance, made up of multiple, minute parts, each of which, in operation, delivers resources to or places constraints upon the operation of another.

So far, we might summarize the argument in this section by suggesting that, if set against Tönnies's *Gemeinschaft/Gesellschaft* dichotomy, the modern state appears to lie very much at the Gesellschaft end of it.[21*] Yet this obvious (if not very useful) characterization raises some objections, the import of which might be summarized by arguing that there is something *gemeinschaftlich* about the state!

To begin with, how plausible is the notion of the state's being "made" or being "built"? Who would be doing the "making" or "building"? One might answer, "a national society"—that is, a geographically, linguistically, ethnically, and culturally distinctive population seeking a political guarantee and expression of its distinctiveness. Yet in many cases such an entity cannot be shown to have existed prior to or even at the time of its alleged state-making activities. For instance, French absolutism "made" the French nation *at least* as much as the French nation "made" the modern French state.

Furthermore, the concrete historical processes leading to the emergence of a state have typically been protracted, tentative, and circuitous, and have presented a wide discrepancy between *undertakings* and *outcomes*. Similar aspects or phases of these processes have received, in different circumstances, widely different justifications and interpretations by the participants—an appeal here to dynastic interests, there to national integrity, there again to the need to create larger markets. All this makes doubtful the "state-building" imagery, the notion that the historical events involved actualized a conscious purpose, an explicit design.

More significantly, both the processes whereby the state emerges and the state-in-being often evoke in the individual participants emotional resonances, depths of commitment and involvement, that are more gemeinschaftlich than gesellschaftlich. They seem to involve, from time to time, a rejection of instrumental, utilitarian, "engineerlike" reasoning; a search for self-transcendence; a surrender to an elevating, spiritual, supraindividual identity. Even Hermann Heller—for a German, an unusually matter-of-fact scholar —argues that "by his will or otherwise the individual finds himself implicated in the state with vitally significant levels of his whole being. . . . The state organization reaches deep into the personal existence of man, forms his being."[22] And Max Weber, whose "Politics as a Vocation" well conveys (often to the dismay of his liberal-minded readers) the *fascinosum et tremendum*, the titanic and demoniac aspects of political experience, goes so far as to attribute to the larger political entities, including of course the modern state, an ability they share only with religion—to impart meaning to death. The warrior's death on the battlefield, Weber suggests, is a consecrated one, a consummation vibrant with elevating feeling.[23] Has not the nineteenth-century state appealed all too often and all too successfully to such motifs in order to send young men willingly to die (and to kill)?

The view, too, that the state is gesellschaftlich because it is "functionally specific," the product of a process of differentiation that in the end focuses all state activities on *only one* aspect or dimension of social life, cannot easily be squared with some implications of the notion of sovereignty insidiously developed by Carl Schmitt. If the state is seen as attending to the *paramount, ultimate* social interest (preserving the collectivity's very existence and integrity), and if in the pursuit of this interest the state can even send its citizens to untimely and painful death, surely there is something conditional, not to say fictional, about its "functional specificity"? Is not the *total* destiny of the collectivity constituted as state, and thus the *totality* of its members' interests, directly affected by the state's demands and fortunes?

Furthermore, the modern state's relation to its citizenry may well appear universalistic, but what of the irreducible particularism deriving from the fact that the world is totally made up of sovereign states, each sharply discriminating between its own citizens and all other human beings, and each binding the former into a fiercely exclusive and demanding bond to itself alone? Finally, the conception of the state as a machine is but a variant of the traditional Anglo-Saxon view of it as merely "a convenience," that is, as a gesellschaftlich reality. But what of the Continental conception of the state as "an entity," as The State? There is little gesellschaftlich about that.

I see no reason to draw from these objections the conclusion that the state is a Gemeinschaft after all. Perhaps all they do is emphasize the inherent limitations of Tönnies's dichotomy, particularly when applied to the larger social forms. An alternative conclusion can perhaps be drawn from something Weber wrote in 1916: "When one says that the state is the highest and ultimate thing in the world, that is entirely correct once it is properly understood. For the state is the highest power organization on earth, it has power over life and death. . . . A mistake comes in, however, when one speaks of the state alone and not of the nation."[24] This passage suggests that the state is indeed gesellschaftlich, and that those aspects appearing to refute this characterization are best taken as referring not to the state as such but to a wider reality (whether or not one wants to follow Weber in designating that reality "the nation"). In this argument, the state is a purposefully constructed, functionally specific machine, but one appealing to and mobilizing deeper and more demanding feelings and emotions to the extent that it serves a more inclusive and less artificial reality.

Legal-Rational Legitimacy

As a system of rule, the state confronts the problem of legitimacy. That is, it wants citizens to comply with its authority not from the inertia of unreasoning routine or the utilitarian calculation of personal advantage, but from the conviction that compliance is right. To this end, each system of rule must put forward understandings that, once shared by the citizens, will impart to its commands a quality of moral obligation. As Max Weber has it, there are three basic types of such understandings, characterizing traditional, charismatic, and legal-rational legitimacy, respectively. Only the last of these is appropriate to the modern state. In this type, a claim to morally motivated obedience is attached to individual commands by virtue of the fact—ascertainable through juristic reasoning—that they are issued in conformity with valid general norms. In turn, the validity of the norms is based on their having been produced according to procedural rules vested in the state's constitution.[25]

Thus, the moral ideal that ultimately legitimizes the modern state is the taming of power through the depersonalization of its exercise. Where power is generated and regulated through general laws, the chance of its arbitrary exercise is minimized; correspondingly minimized is the element of personal submission in the relations of individuals at large to those exercising faculties of rule, since the latter only exercise rule as occupants of specified and legally controlled positions. At bottom, in their political relations individuals obey not one another but the law.

In the modern state the relation between the state and the law is particularly close. The law is no longer conceived as an assemblage of immemorially evolved, customary jural rules, or of corporatively held, traditional prerogatives and immunities; nor is it conceived as the expression of principles of justice resting on the will of God or the dictates of "Nature" to which the state is simply expected to lend the sanction of its powers of enforcement. Modern law is instead a body of enacted laws; it is *positive* law, willed, made, and given validity by the state itself in the exercise of its sovereignty, mostly through public, documented, generally recent decisions.[26]

In fact, according to some nineteenth-century (and early twentieth-century) constructions, there is a relation of near-identity between the state and its law. Law-free areas are allowed in a few of the state's activities, particularly with reference to strictly political interests (external security, the keeping of public order), or to narrowly matter-of-fact, nonnormative considerations of necessity or convenience in administration; but these areas themselves must be enumerated and circumscribed by law. In any case, within the system of rule the law is the state's standard mode of expression, its very language, the essential medium of its activity. One can visualize the whole state as a *legally* arranged set of organs for the framing, application, and enforcement of *laws*.

Continental legal theory and practice see this latter aspect of the state's relation to law as embodied in the first half of the conventional partition of state law into public and private law (though all law is state law). As I suggested in the last section, the state is constituted and operates as a formal organization; within it individuals and their decisions represent and actualize the competences and faculties of organs and offices. But for this to be the case, general rules must establish and regulate such competences and faculties, and the operations expressing them. The state's constant preoccupation with the coordination and direction of its own actions requires again the formulation and enforcement of general rules defining standards for such actions, stating the considerations relevant to them, and so forth. A vast body of public law comes into being as a result of this indispensable process of making rules, laying down directives, establishing criteria, dictating orientations of action: "Law is technically (not always politically) the most accomplished form of domination, since typically and in the long run it makes possible the most precise and effective orientation and ordering of political activity, and the most secure calculation and imputation of the conduct that constitutes and actualizes the state's power." [27]

The other half of the partition, private law, does not give directives for the operation of state organs but rather sets frameworks for the autonomous activity of individuals pursuing their own private interests. Insofar as individuals see it as in their interest to enter into relations with one another, the state provides through legislation the means whereby, if necessary, those individuals can secure the interest in question by calling upon the state's judicial and law-enforcement apparatus. By making such provisions the state determines (generally, and on the face of it impartially) which classes of interests are worthy of its support. It sets out the conditions under which those interests may be pursued—for instance, the degree of mental maturity and awareness required for the individual to commit his resources, the standards of good faith to be observed in transactions, and the formalities required to make transactions binding—and establishes the consequences that will derive from transactions involved in that pursuit. Moreover, the state establishes the duties and prerogatives following from the possession of property and other rights, or following from such statuses as spouse, heir, or guardian.

Insofar as they fulfill the conditions laid down in general terms by such laws, individuals are said to possess rights, duties, and obligations; they can produce, or must submit to, determinate modifications in their mutual relations. The rules indicated above, and others that complement them, obviously all express the state's authority vis-à-vis its citizens; but they are designed to support and control the individual's search for his own advantage by making precise and predictable his relations to other individuals and thus rendering the interplay of "antagonistic cooperators" transparent, calculable, and noncoercive.

Constitutional Guarantees

The prevalently liberal, antiauthoritarian inspiration of the nineteenth-century constitutional state is revealed in two overlapping arrangements that are typical of its public law.

In the first place, since all positive law is changeable, there is a danger that new legislation may destroy vested rights or disturb the holders of such rights in their peaceable and unrestricted enjoyment of them. To guard against this, some substantive legal principles are enshrined in a special, higher legal standing as "constitutional" enactments; laws violating or limiting such principles are denied validity, or are recognized as valid only if particularly demanding procedural requirements are met in framing them.

In the second place, citizens are vested with rights in the public sphere just as they are in the private one (again, mostly through constitutional enactments). State organs, including in some cases legislative organs, are directly prohibited from encroaching on those rights. Furthermore, as we shall see in a moment, some of those rights allow individual citizens fulfilling eligibility requirements to monitor and take part in the formation of public decisions, particularly the enactment of laws (through elections and representative legislatures) and judicial proceedings (through the institution of the jury). In this way the individual citizen is "plugged into" the operations of the state, in however mediated a fashion; this is intended to afford him a guarantee both of his rights against abuse and of his legitimate interests against disregard by public organs.

Habermas classifies as follows the rights that nineteenth-century constitutions and similar enactments most frequently attribute to the individual: rights pertaining to the sphere of what he calls "the reasoning public" (freedoms of speech, opinion, assembly, association) and pertaining to the political prerogatives of private individuals (electoral rights, rights of petition, etc.); rights making up the status of the individual as a free person (inviolability of his residence, his correspondence, etc.; prohibition of transactions disposing of personal freedom); and rights referring to the transactions of private property owners in the sphere of the civil society (equality before the law, freedom from control, protection of private property, protection of rights to inheritance, etc.).[28]

Now these rights had more positive implications than the somewhat negative one of bounding the state's power to make laws.[29*] This latter significance flowed from the intent of *committing the state legally to its own laws*, something very different from, and not easily brought into accord with, the point previously made that the law was the state's very language, the chief medium of its functioning. For that notion entailed that the state could "speak" or produce *any* law at all; and it was exactly that intrinsic changeability of the law that was dangerous, from the liberal viewpoint.

But placing legally valid boundaries around positive law was logically impossible. The constitution might "bind" normal legislation, and the latter establish safeguards of the citizens' rights (public and private) "binding" in turn upon the executive and the judiciary; but the constitution itself was a piece, however exalted, of positive legislation, and as such it was inherently modifiable whatever the restrictions. To deal with this quandary, political and legal theorists used various devices—for instance, ideas drawn from the notion of natural law (such as the existence of rights of *man* prior to and above those of the citizen), or interpretations of constitution-framing reminiscent of the theory of social contract. But these attempted solutions contrasted with the prevalently secular and progress-minded temper of the times, which in "legal positivism" had celebrated a victory over natural-law and social-contract theories. Besides, these latter theories had egalitarian implications that made them an awkward weapon for the bourgeoisie to use.

Ultimately, even such a vigorous and lucid thinker as Georg Jellinek (a close associate of Max Weber at Heidelberg at the end of the nineteenth century, and an outstanding public-law theorist) was reduced to pleading his own firm—but not satisfactorily argued—conviction that the state was indeed *bound* by and to its own law and *had* to respect certain rights of the citizen.[30] In the following passage, I have emphasized places where the weakness of his reasoning seems to me particularly apparent.

Criminal law does not simply give directions to the judge; tax law does not simply give instructions to the tax inspector. They entail an assurance given the subjects that such laws will be followed. All norms establish an expectation that, *unless a legally valid reason for their suspension obtains*, they will be complied with [by public officials]. . . . Without such assurance, the individual would not be able to calculate his own action and its consequences. . . . As it creates law, the state obliges itself vis-à-vis the subjects to apply and enforce such law.

The personalities (whether individuals or groups) that operate within the state possess rights of their own, not at the discretion of or as a concession from the sovereign state, nor as the state's delegates. *They possess their rights because they are considered as carriers of rights*, as persons—a quality that it is wholly outside the real power of the state to take away from them.[31]

As this last sentence shows, the ultimate guarantee of the state's respect for the individual's rights, since it cannot be either juridical (if circular reasoning is to be avoided) or metaphysical (since natural-law and similar constructions have been discarded), must be sociological; hence the reference to "the real power" of the state. There is nothing wrong with that, except that Jellinek's is very poor sociology: it is in fact wholly within "the real power" of the state to treat individuals otherwise than as the carriers of rights. This was clear from pre-nineteenth-century systems of rule, about which Jellinek knew a great deal. Nonetheless, he disregarded that evidence, presumably because he did not think of those systems as "proper" states. He seems to have felt (though he could not satisfactorily argue) that somehow by its very nature the state as it had come to full realization in the late-eighteenth and nineteenth centuries *was unable to do* certain things.

Let us now return briefly to the problem of legitimacy, with which we started this section. Referring to Weber's typology of legitimacy, Carl Schmitt argues that the modern state's (and Weber's) emphasis on *legality*—that is, on the observance of stated procedural rules for the formation and execution of the state's decisions—does not so much embody a distinctive type of legitimacy (as Weber himself thought) as dispense with legitimacy proper, supplant it.[32] The very idea of legitimacy, according to Schmitt, refers to some idea of moral goodness, to some intrinsically valid and commanding substantive ideal that somehow communicates validity to individual commands seen as reflecting it; whereas the procedural rules that supposedly validate commands under "legal-rational legitimacy" are purely formal and do not possess and cannot communicate any intrinsic rightness, and thus any authentic legitimacy, to commands ultimately grounded in them. (It might be argued that Weber himself conceded this when he distinguished between *formal* and *material* legal rationality, only the former being seen as characteristic of modern legal systems.)

One must concede some force to Carl Schmitt's argument. Yet it seems to me that within Western culture, at any rate, the principle of the depersonalization of power—which I have suggested is entailed in the Weberian notion of legal-rational legitimacy—does possess a distinctive moral significance, and thus a true, if perhaps weak, legitimizing force. So does the notion, embodied in the characteristic liberal preference for having collective decisions emerge from the public confrontation of opinion in open-ended debate, that as far as possible law should be the product of *ratio* (reason) rather than of *voluntas* (will). This involves a distinctive moral design whereby, in the words of Hegel, the validity of law is made to rest "no longer upon force, nor primarily upon habits and mores, but upon insights and arguments."[33]

Significant Features of the Political Process

In the early phases of the development of the modern state, as we have seen, the prime theme of the internal political process was the tug-of-war among autonomous power centers (individual or corporate, secular or ecclesiastical) over the extent and security of their respective jurisdictional prerogatives and immunities.

Following up the achievements of absolutism, the nineteenth-century state appears to have settled *this* political issue by institutionalizing the principle we have previously called "unity" or "internal sovereignty." Now the main internal political issue becomes the content and direction of the powers of rule monopolized by the state, especially as they bear on the distribution of the national product and on the control over the means of its production. In the next section I shall divide that issue into a number of component ones; here, though, I want to point up some broad features of the internal political process in the nineteenth-century state.

"Civility." Rulership always entails control over means of coercion. In comparison with other systems of rule, the nineteenth-century state builds up this aspect of rule by strengthening its monopoly of legitimate coercion, and by making coercion technically more sophisticated and more formidable. However, it also differentiates and separates coercion from other aspects of the internal political process, which results in that process becoming more "civil."

Within the increasingly vast and ramified apparatus of the state, only two sectors of the executive branch—the military and the police—remain directly concerned with coercion. But the key decisions about their organization and financing, and about the deployment of their might, are vested in *other* organs (legislative, executive). Thus legitimate coercion becomes a less diffuse, pervasive, and visible, and a more controlled and specialized aspect of rule. (For that matter, a similar reduction in the visible sway of coercion can be observed in social life at large. In particular, the dominant capitalist mode of production does not involve the direct use of coercion.)

Another manifestation of "civility" is the widespread adoption, over the entire Europe-centered system of states, of more humane forms of criminal prosecution and punishment. Furthermore, under normal conditions, violent forms of political expression become less frequent. Following the lead of England, many states institutionalize opposition to the current political leadership or to current policies, and make the occupancy of many political posts the object of regulated, peaceable competition. The "public rights" discussed above make possible organized dissent, and the constitutional removal of certain issues from the political arena—particularly religious issues, which in the past had been highly inflammatory—reduces the scope and intensity of that dissent.

The legislative organs, which normally operate as the visible seat of the state's sovereignty, function essentially as "talking shops" under elaborate, formal rules for ordering debate; they are increasingly peopled by members of the professional and business classes, men mostly of relatively peaceable dispositions. Both here and even more within administrative organs, men trained in the law are increasingly in the majority among those transacting the day-to-day business of the state. Thus that business is generally dealt with in a sober, discursive manner; the state is run increasingly on the basis of matter-of-fact judgment and sophisticated, trained reasoning, and less and less on the basis of brawn, ceremonial pomp, and warlike display.

As against this internal civility, let us remember that such wars as are fought between states become more and more massive and murderous; moreover, their occurrence awakens and expresses, in ever wider circles among the population, passions of unusual and frightening ferocity. Also, in those colonial dependencies that constitute an integral part of the productive system of many Western states, systematic and brutal coercion plays an open and direct role, not just in keeping native populations under subjection but in exploiting them economically. Finally, internally the state some-times deploys openly and harshly its potential for coercion—in particular when political dissent or the resistance to exploitation of subaltern strata seem to threaten the internal allocation of politi-cal and economic power. In such circumstances even the distinc-tion between the military and the police is often violated; the army is brought in to break strikes, put down riots, and sometimes take over the policing of whole regions.[34]

Plurality of foci. Though unitarily constituted, the nineteenth-century state is also articulated into many organs and offices, with varied competences and concerns. Thus the political process be-comes correspondingly differentiated; it becomes focused around a number of organs, layers of regulation, issues, organized bodies of opinion, and sets of collective interests. The many nodes and junc-tions of the system's structure offer many points of entry into the process.

In the hope of exercising leverage on the formation of policy, progressively wider sections of the population become involved in the political process; and their increasing participation in turn generates many, often overlapping alignments. For instance, the array of interests, views, and people competing for power and in-fluence at the national level generally differs from that at the regional or municipal level. The alignments of opinion on foreign-policy issues often cut across those focused on fiscal, welfare, or educational policies.

Open-endedness. We have seen that in earlier stages of the state's development individuals and bodies typically voiced *traditional* claims to take part in the political process, and articulated demands largely by appealing to time-hallowed privileges. Thus their strug-gles, persistent and bitter as they were, went on under the assump-tion that there had existed in the past and could be restored in the present a condition of balance among their various privileges and claims.

No such assumption applies to the nineteenth-century state. Here political business is transacted (continuously and publicly) by reference not to traditional, differentiated, autonomously held prerogatives of the parties, but to the open-ended potential of the unitary power of the state, a thoroughly secular entity capable in principle of indefinite elaboration, definition, and expansion. As we have also seen, positive law, the state's very language, is intrinsically changeable and can orient and empower an indefinite variety of acts of rule.

The political process has accordingly become oriented to abstract, ever-receding targets—be they the promotion of the state's power in the comity of nations, the people's welfare, or the individual's pursuit of happiness. In the name of these targets (as they are defined and mutually adjusted through the political contest), changes may legitimately be made at any time in the balance of individual and collective interests.

Even leaving aside the dynamic character of the society it complements, such a political system must of necessity always be generating new themes for public concern and for authoritative action. Accordingly, it tends to require for its functioning ever new resources, ever new faculties and facilities of rule to be applied to its open-ended aims.

Controversy. What I have just called open-endedness is not a peculiarity of the nineteenth-century state; as Tocqueville's *Ancien Régime* shows, it was already well in evidence in late-absolutist France, with its urge to push back continually the boundaries of state action, to regulate ever-newer aspects and areas of social business. However, the "ancien régime" was semidespotic. It possessed no constituted arena for public discussion and control of the state's action, which received all its impulses from above. The nineteenth-century state, on the other hand, is constructed in a way that does not just allow but requires public debate, the confrontation of opinion. Conflict, however bounded; controversy, however regulated—these are features not incidental but essential to the operation of the political system.[35]

The centrality of representative institutions. Many of the characteristics already discussed—for instance the key significance of law and the role of controversy in its formation—find expression in the central position of representative institutions in the nineteenth-century political process. Naturally, what I call "centrality" is a matter of degree—and thus of conflict. Parliament is obviously more central to a parliamentary system of government than either to a presidential system or to one where the personal confidence of a monarch, not the political composition of the legislature, decides who is to lead the executive. Yet it is necessarily in parliament (however organized) that laws are formed; moreover, parliament represents the public realm par excellence, not merely as an arena for discussion but as the seat of vital decision-making processes.

Parliament must mediate between the "severalness" of individually held opinions (each secured some expression by "public rights") and the need for univocal, general commands to resolve and reduce the diversity of those opinions. To do this, parliament cannot function purely as a condensed reflection of the distribution of opinion within the public; it must also *simplify* that distribution, *focus* it on issues, and *generate* alignments, majorities, and oppositions. Parliament must, at the same time, "couple" and "uncouple" the society and the state—the former as the locus where private individuals freely form and express views and preferences, the latter as a machine for framing and executing binding commands.

To this end, each member of parliament is seen as empowered by an open-ended mandate issuing not from individual voters or even his entire particular constituency but from the politically significant public at large. He is expected to join a relatively stable alignment of like-minded fellow members, and it is understood that to this end he will have to play down some of his personal views and play up some of those the alignment holds in common. To the same end, most parliaments have a fixed or at any rate relatively lengthy duration in a given composition in order to allow the members to distance themselves from the all-too-fluid developments of opinion in the broader public and either to "lead" those developments or to "lag behind" them. The spectrum of opinion and of political will that parliament represents is necessarily narrower than that within the electorate; it is further reduced by compromises and alliances, and above all by the tendency for controversy in parliament to become focused on the formation of a majority, on the contrast between "ins" and "outs."

In all these ways parliament acquires autonomy vis-à-vis the broad public, and maintains, or seeks to acquire, primacy with respect to the executive. Parliament is central to the system because it does not simply *transmit* political impulses originating elsewhere; it *produces* political impulses by processing the orientations of the electorate it represents. It is central, too, in that by commenting on and criticizing actions of government and ongoing social developments it feeds information back to the electorate and thereby increases the people's awareness of public issues and both the choices those issues open and the burdens and opportunities they involve. Finally, it is central because and insofar as it forms and selects *leaders*—individuals capable of formulating issues, projecting solutions, voicing and forming public opinion, taking responsibility.[36]

Significant Classes of Political Issues

I shall attempt here only the sketchiest classification of the most significant classes of issues that come most frequently and materially to the fore in the nineteenth-century state.

Constitutional issues. Among these issues we find the question of whether the head of state should be an elected president or a hereditary monarch, and of what his specific powers should be. We also find the issues of the distribution of powers between legislative, executive, and judicial organs, and the allocation of tasks and resources to central and local administrative organs. Finally, we find a variety of issues concerning the relations between state and church(es), the constitutional position of the army, and the extension of the franchise.

Foreign-policy issues. The "little versus great England" debate is the most sharply contoured and exemplary among these, involving as it does questions of alliances, tariffs, armaments, and tempos and directions of colonial expansion. These are, indeed, the central issues of the nineteenth-century states system, and bring about its disastrous collapse in 1914.

The "social question." In the nineteenth century this expression designated a set of issues arising from the commercialization and industrialization of national economies. It concerned such disparate phenomena as demographic pressure; proletarianization of the subaltern strata; urban epidemics; criminality; destitution; industrial accidents; mass de-Christianization; the growth of organized unionism and socialism; illiteracy; "vice" in the form of prostitution, juvenile delinquency, illegitimacy, alcoholism, etc.; social rootlessness and political subversiveness; and strikes and unemployment.

It was by no means universally accepted that all such issues (or any such, according to some currents of opinion) were *political*, in the sense that state activities other than purely police ones ought to be brought to bear upon them. But as we shall see in the next chapter, a number of these issues became progressively locked into the political process largely by (1) the enfranchisement of social groups that expected the state to attend to such issues, (2) the resulting emergence of the notion of "social" rights of citizenship, and (3) the assumption by the state of some responsibility for ameliorating the phenomena in question. But the decisions involved in this protracted development were contested bitterly and widely. Within the complex story of the relations between liberalism, democracy, and socialism in the nineteenth century, much revolved around those decisions.

Issues of economic management. The state's action concerning the "social question" may perhaps be considered as the more dramatic and visible aspect of the role it played in the latter part of the nineteenth century in sustaining and advancing capitalism and in allocating the national product among various claimant interests. Another, less conspicuous set of issues bearing essentially on the same problem might be labeled "issues of economic management."

The reason why these issues (and the attendant state action) *were* less conspicuous is twofold. First, through most of the nineteenth century in most states public action on these matters consisted largely of the construction and management of legal, fiscal, monetary, and financial frameworks for the *autonomous*, self-regulating operations of the allocative mechanisms constituted by the markets for land, labor, and capital. Second, the state played a positive, but again relatively unobtrusive role in the accumulation and reproduction of capital, and in the moderation of economic imbalances that the market system could not adequately control. This second type of action involved such diverse things as the granting of land to railway companies; the floating and servicing of the national debt; the erection of tariff walls; the granting of patents and of corporate prerogatives to firms; the public financing of major industrial undertakings; the repression, containment, or regulation of unions and of collective bargaining; and the overt or covert diplomatic, military, and financial backing of colonial undertakings.

It might be suggested that the four classes of issues we have discussed in this section represent for the nineteenth-century state the legacy of different phases in its historical development. In a sense, the constitutional issues project into the unitary framework of the nineteenth-century state those disputes over the allocation of independent powers of rule that we have seen were most actively carried on under the feudal and ständisch systems of rule. The foreign-policy issues revolve around the implications for the nineteenth-century state of the states system consecrated originally by the Peace of Westphalia. And we may view what I have called the issues of economic management as the legacy of absolutist mercantilism, however modified and disguised by the liberal theory and practice prevalent in the nineteenth century.

However, the issues making up the "social question" are almost wholly new in their multiplicity, intractability, and political significance. They are in fact placed upon the state's agenda largely by the workings of the capitalist mode of production as it enters its advanced industrial phase; they thus reflect the ever-increasing hold of that mode of production on the totality of social life in the nineteenth-century West. In fact, the dominance of the capitalist mode of production can be seen as largely dictating the form in which all the other classes of issues are posed and at the same time limiting the range of their possible solutions. The issues of economic management, at any rate in the states where capitalism reached its industrial phase relatively early, had to be confronted within the framework set by the institutions of private enterprise and the market, and by the logic of capital accumulation; these elements necessarily excluded the mercantilist emphasis on bullion, state enterprise, and authoritative regulation of business activities. The *private* nature of the dominant economic interests, and their apparently uncoercive relation to the subaltern ones, set limits to the constitutional struggles; these, as I have indicated, developed accordingly as a contest over the access to and the exercise of influence upon the organs of (unitary) state power, and did *not* take the form of open claims for the appropriation of political prerogatives. Finally, interstate tensions are moderated to a point, and heightened beyond that point, by becoming focused on the competition, among metropolitan centers of capital accumulation, over the markets and resources of nonstate or pseudostate areas of the world.

But if it is true, as I have suggested, that the dominant mode of production largely shaped the agenda of state action itself and the attendant political contrasts, clearly this points to a close relation of complementarity between the nineteenth-century state and the bourgeois civil society of the time. The import of this relation and its modifications in the twentieth century are the themes of my final chapter.

CHAPTER VI

State and Society Under Liberalism
and After

IF WE CONSIDER together the imposing institutional edifice discussed in the last chapter and the society that the advance of the capitalist mode of production generated in the West in the late-eighteenth and nineteenth centuries, we may be struck at first by the differences in the institutional principles and in the nature of the interests typically operating in each. The state is first and foremost a unitary entity. Externally, in its pursuit of advantage vis-à-vis other sovereign states, it obeys an imperious "reason" of its own, inapplicable to any other social pursuit. Internally, it speaks the abstract and general language of law, making and enforcing decisions supposedly oriented to nondivisive, widely shared interests, assembling unto itself all faculties and facilities of rule, and recognizing no subject as its equal, except in its external relations.

The society, on the other hand, appears as a vast, though bounded, multitude of discrete, self-interested, and self-activated individuals relating to one another primarily through private choice. Such relations may generate legally enforceable effects, but these are deemed to be the individual's responsibility, to rest on his autonomous ability to obligate himself in exchange for benefits sought. Furthermore, the actual enforcement of such effects, though initiated by individuals in their own interest (typically through court actions), is not the individual's business but the state's. For as we have seen, in the modern state individuals as such cannot exercise on one another powers of rule, and must recognize one another as juridically free and equal. Their mutual relations are unceasingly structured and destructured by the myriad impacts of their interested choices and expressions of preference through the neutral, automatic operations of the market and of the forums of opinion and taste.

For individuals so conceived, the activation of their public as against their private capacities—the shift from the concerns of *homo oeconomicus* to those of the citizen—constitutes a radical reorientation of the self, an arduous feat of self-transcendence. To make this possible, as we have seen, complex and sophisticated political arrangements both "couple" and "uncouple" society and the state. Tocqueville claimed to have seen the Americans perform that feat frequently and easily, especially by participating in voluntary civic associations.[1] And it could be argued that within the sphere of society itself increasing institutional differentiation required of most individuals role-shifts of nearly comparable magnitude on a day-to-day basis. The transition from acquisitive businessman to devoted father or husband, for example, was nearly as radical as that from businessman to member of a civic organization.

Marx, however, was not far wrong in his bloody-minded suspicion that the duty imposed on the members of the "civil society" periodically to experience "ecstasies"[2]—to sublimate away their mundane, egoistic interests in order to act as citizens—was at best a high-flown idealistic abstraction, at worst a deceitful cover for substantial continuities and congruities between the interests pursued in each sphere. Whether despite or because of the differences in their institutional principles, state and society in the liberal era were in fact intrinsically compatible, were indeed necessarily complementary realities. What is more, in the liberal design the state was to be an instrumentality of the society rather than vice versa—an instrumentality specialized in the exercise of rule *over* the society. If this conception involves an implicit contradiction (How can the state both serve the society and rule over it?), the explanation for it lies in the fact that the society was not a fused but a split reality.

Essentially, the liberal state was constructed to favor and sustain through its acts of rule the class domination of the bourgeoisie over the society as a whole. This was the end to which the institutional principles of the state were ultimately directed, as it was the reason for their apparent contrast with those of the society. For example, the state attached to all individuals abstractly equal faculties for freely disposing of their own resources; the reason for this was that the capitalist mode of production required labor power to be sold for wages through individual employment contracts. Again, the state was enjoined from interfering in the market, except in such generalized ways as by regulating the money system or the machinery for the enforcement of contracts; the reason for this was that the nineteenth-century market was capable of doing on its own terms nearly all the allocating that needed to be done, and in doing so automatically directed the processes of production and accumulation to the advantage of capital owners. The equality of all individuals before the law made sense as a constitutional principle because as a matter of course the legal protection of private property directed the order-keeping, law enforcement, and repressive activities of police and courts to favor the interests of the propertied groups.[3] The distinctive features of modern law as a body of stated rules, Habermas argues, reflect the specific moral and cultural preferences of the bourgeoisie: such rules allow a free ambit to bourgeois "inwardness" because they are external, to bourgeois individuality because they are general, to bourgeois subjectivity because they are objective, and to bourgeois concreteness because they are abstract.[4]

In sum, in Habermas's view, as in other Marx-inspired critical interpretations of the state/society distinction, the state's institutional principles are instrumental to bourgeois class dominance within the society; political structures are primarily responsive to the requirements of the capitalist mode of production, at the same time expressing and concealing the functional subordination of political to economic power.[5] Such arguments strike me as correct but somewhat partial. After all, the state/society distinction did not *originate* from the relationship between political and economic power. It had earlier found fundamental expression in the slow but inexorable disentanglement of the Western state from the Church(es) and Christianity through the tortuous story that leads from *cuius regio eius religio* through religious tolerance and freedom of conscience to the "secular state." In this story, it would seem, not economic interests but *raison d'état* and a momentous, autonomous development in religious awareness and in moral consciousness played a critical role. Matters of creed and cult, not of property and contract, had been the first to be claimed as "private" with respect to the state, as proper for the state to ignore or to safeguard impartially.

Yet momentous as it had been, the religious dimension of the state/society distinction had set over against the state a social force —the militant Christianity of Protestant Reformation and Catholic Counter-Reformation—that despite its surface vigor was historically *recessive*. When that distinction was later institutionalized, the state's counterpart was on the contrary an *ascendant* force, inherently dynamic and powerfully expansive—whether one calls it Money, the Economy, the Market, or Capital. One can recognize that in the story of the "separation" between state and society the religious aspect had operated early, independently, and significantly, and yet accept the Marxian view to the extent of recognizing that the economic aspect entailed for the state itself a much more serious challenge. Whereas religion, once separated from the state, was to confront it with progressively fewer and weaker claims, the capitalist economy was in a position largely to dictate the terms and determine the significance of its own separation from the state.

To put it another way, under capitalism the economy does not operate within the societal sphere simply as one "factor" among and coordinate with others; rather, it imperiously *sub*ordinates or otherwise reduces the independent significance of all other factors, including religion, the family, the status system, education, technology, science, and the arts. The capitalist mode of production gains an ever wider and firmer hold on the social process at large; "exchange values" progressively drive out "use values"; all manner of human interests are processed through the market and subjected to its rules. To phrase the point with Marx, the "political economy" constitutes not one aspect or phase but "the anatomy" itself of the civil society.[6]

To see what challenge this entailed for the state, it is enough to point out that the state's social mission had often been seen (for instance, in the Hegelian tradition) as involving the homogenizing and hegemonizing, as it were, of a society conceived as inherently fragmented, atomized, and centerless. Yet with so much "homogenizing and hegemonizing" in fact done by the capitalist economic system, what is left for the state to do? Will its institutional separation from the society allow it enough leverage to maintain its autonomy, or perhaps even to "fight back" and gain a hold over the economic process itself?

These questions suggest two contestants struggling for superiority while each maintaining a separate identity and a firm base in its distinctive territory. However, the imagery I develop in this chapter chiefly envisages rather the progressive compenetration of the two territories, the displacement and erosion of the line separating state from society. I shall restate and synthesize familiar arguments according to which the institutional differentiation between sociocultural and economic processes on the one hand and political processes on the other, which was characteristic of the West in the nineteenth century, has largely ceased to operate in our own. However, the state still functions in our time within and through political and juridical *forms* derived from the liberal-democratic nineteenth-century constitution; it does so to an extent sufficient partly to disguise and partly to limit the changes in the *substance* of the political process, but at the same time it modifies and distorts the forms themselves.[7]

In a later section I shall take as an example of this last point the inexorable but formally concealed displacement of elected legislatures from the center of the state. But before discussing this consequence of the compenetration of the political and societal realms, we must consider a range of phenomena that may be viewed as causes and/or manifestations of that development.

The Pressure of Collective Interests

I shall consider first, in this section and the two that follow, some pressures on the state/society line that have originated from the society side and have led to a greater involvement between state and society than the classical constitutional model allowed for. I shall focus on phenomena reflecting the evolving dynamic of the capitalist economic system.

Capitalism is a system of power. It entails the self-perpetuating dominance of the capital-owning class over those social groups whose livelihood and social standing depend on the sale of labor power; and to this extent it generates contrasting sets of typical interests in the two key classes. The safest way to uphold this central facet of modern Western society in the sphere of the state is to exclude from the constitutional political process the claims and demands of groups in whose interest it may lie to abolish capital ownership, to modify its distribution, or to interfere with its chances for profit or its control over accumulation.

In the nineteenth and early twentieth centuries, the chief means of excluding from the political arena groups whose interests might be incompatible with the maintenance and prosperity of the capitalist system was the restriction of suffrage.[8] Without the franchise, such groups were limited to the exercise of civil rights having no direct political significance, or to unconstitutional forms of political dissent containable through police and other repressive action. Once incompatible interests were "filtered out" of the political process in this way, public institutions, and signally parliament, could attend to the resolution of such contrasting interests as were generated within the framework of capitalist-bourgeois institutions and values.[9] The rights to vote and to hold office were accordingly restricted to men possessing property and/or educational qualifications. The justification for this took the line that the ability to deliberate on distinctively public and political concerns (directly or through representatives) in an enlightened and critical manner could only be imputed to individuals possessing a stake in the market system—entrepreneurs, professionals, rentiers, at most the more established self-employed workers. We might say, to use again Marx's ironic image, that to experience "ecstasies," to jump as it were out of one's own private skin into the lofty forum where an informed and public-spirited citizenry agitated issues of general significance, one needed a secure platform in a proper home, with a duly constituted and patriarchally run family, a respectable patrimony, a capital to risk, or sophisticated skills to put to independent use.[10]

It matters little whether or not we take seriously these arguments and their multiple variants in liberal thinking. The point is that the disfranchised themselves took them seriously. It was expressly in order to bring into the political arena interests in contrast to and not easily "balanceable" with those of the capital-owning class that they sought the franchise, eventually gained it, and used it (with varying success) to bring the state's power to bear on their condition and to reduce or ameliorate their economic inferiority.[11] For various reasons, the subaltern strata could not long be prevented from obtaining the franchise and seeking to put it to their own use. The growing fiscal and military needs of the state were leading it to engage ever-larger numbers of the masses in an increasingly direct relation to itself; and some degree of legitimate participation in the country's political process suggested itself as a counterpart to burdens imposed.[12] Also, the possession by the masses of basic civil rights, which we have seen was required by the capitalist mode of production, gave the disfranchised a toehold in the larger society and a means of taking part in "public activities" to the end of gaining political rights.[13] Similarly, an increasingly sophisticated industrial technology made at least minimum literacy a requisite of the work force; but the resulting establishment of public education systems constituted an encroachment on the state/society line and increased the workers' ability to organize and mobilize themselves. Finally, where even a rudimentary party system involving competition for votes existed, the "outs" were often led to promote the enlargement of the electorate in order to be rewarded at the polls by the newly enfranchised.[14]

The existence of the liberal "public realm," where issues could be debated and associations formed among individuals sharing interests and views, was used not only by the lower classes to agitate for electoral rights but by both privileged and underprivileged economic actors to organize coalitions to further their economic and status advantage. The operations of these coalitions—typically trade unions and employers' associations—introduce elements of coercion and "bargaining" into the processes allocating the social product between labor and capital or between different sections of each. This in turn has the effect of modifying or suspending the classical rules according to which markets are supposed to operate (through unplanned, mechanical adjustments among myriad individual choices). The impact of this development on the state/society line can be seen in the fact that the rules on such matters as collective bargaining and union membership, together with much legislation dealing with "welfare," form a corpus (labeled "labor," "industrial," or "social" law) that straddles the divide between private and public law.

Furthermore, those same coalitions or organizations represent and mobilize interests of such magnitude that they become capable of engaging various state organs in a distinctive game of "pressure" or "interest" politics played outside the public realm and without the mediation of parliament. Thus interests that on the face of it are purely private—since the organizations in question are mostly formed and run under the empire of the common law, without public recognition and control—are found either activating or blocking public policies that directly affect them. They do so with such effectiveness that the state frequently finds it in its own interest to associate such organizations in its own operations,[15] co-opting their leaders into organs deliberating administrative policies, consulting them on legislation, using their facilities to monitor the interests they organize, and expecting them on occasion to discipline their members or curb their demands in order to ensure the success of certain state initiatives.[16] Moreover, in this fashion the allocation of the social product through acts of rule (formally still originating from the state's undivided sovereignty) becomes ostensibly the key issue of the political process. Accordingly, interests of a private nature are either openly given voice in that process, or covertly allowed to affect it, or sometimes offered opportunities to engage in de facto acts of rule themselves.

Capitalist Developments: Effects on the Occupational System

Above, I linked some encroachments on the state/society line with the nature of capitalism in its conceptually minimal form—a productive system where profit is appropriated by a capital-owning class that purchases on the market the labor power of the propertyless. But both those encroachments and others can be seen as deriving from *developments* in the capitalist mode of production—in the structure of the dominant production units, the distribution of capital ownership, and so forth. In particular, the long-term trend toward higher levels of capitalization of industrial enterprises produces, more or less directly, several effects relevant to our argument. A number of these effects are mediated through a changing occupational structure. In particular, a more advanced industrial base requires an increasingly differentiated, literate, skilled, and better-motivated work force. As a result, the composition of the work force changes, and its rising level of education increases its political awareness and leads it to make increasing claims on the action of the state.

Here I should like to focus briefly on occupational changes occurring within middle-class strata—those traditionally associated with the bourgeoise in terms of status, life-style, self-conception, cultural preferences, and political orientation. The key phenomenon is the development of a large employee middle class, whose position in the production system (though not in the consumption system) comes to resemble that of the manual working class. This development has two effects. First, it makes economic self-sufficiency untenable as a suffrage qualification, since increasingly sizeable groups would come to lose the franchise as a result; and we have seen that the trend is toward increasing rather than decreasing the franchise. Second, it leads the employee middle class to imitate and outdo the manual working class in pressing the state to safeguard its "private" interests. It seeks to preserve through state action that economic security and social standing it can no longer ground either on the possession of a family patrimony (see Keynes's "euthanasia of the rentier"), or on the ability to maintain its independence while placing on the market valued, sophisticated services.

Yet even when employee strata find sufficient demand for their services on the labor market, and even when their income allows them to maintain a middle-class standard of living, they still look outside the market system to the state to satisfy their aspirations for security. Habermas outlines the long-term results of these developments as follows in a discussion of their impact on the institutional configuration of the modern urban family:

As the family property becomes reduced to the income from employment of the single breadwinner, the family loses its ability to look after itself in emergencies and to make its own provisions for old age. . . . The risks of unemployment, accident, illness, old age, and death of the breadwinner must be covered largely through welfare provisions of the state. . . . The individual family member relies on public guarantees of its basic requirements, whereas the bourgeois family used to bear the risk privately. Over and above such needs resulting from emergency situations, provisions are also publicly made for various other aspects of existence, from housing to employment services, occupational and educational counseling, the monitoring of health, etc. . . . The bourgeois family, no longer needed as the typical locus of capital formation through savings, increasingly loses also the functions of nurturance and education, protection, moral support and guidance, elementary tradition and orientation. It loses the ability to shape behavior even in the spheres that in the (classical) bourgeois family were considered as the most intimate seat of privacy. In a way, through such public guarantees of its status, the family, this private residuum, becomes itself de-privatized.[17]

As industrialization progresses and raises the standard of living and the expectations of the whole working population, the effects of the phenomena Habermas lists extend beyond the middle-class family to the contemporary Western family at large and have a correspondingly greater impact on the state/society line.

Capitalist Developments: Effects on the Production System

Qualitatively similar but even more massive effects than those discussed above can be traced to changes in the dimensions and structures of the dominant production units as the joint-stock company and the corporation become the protagonists of the expanding industrial economy. To begin with, the very concession of corporate status to the joint economic endeavors of individuals is of doubtful legitimacy in the face of liberal ideology, and has strong preliberal, as well as antiliberal, antecedents.[18] The facts that in American parlance corporations are often labeled "public" (as in "going public"), and that a complex and by no means automatic political-legal decision is required to confer on corporations a legal capacity distinct from that of the individual owners, suggest how awkward such artificial subjects are from the standpoint of the distinction between public and private law. The same point is implicit in the complex (though mostly ineffectual) provisions whereby various governmental or semigovernmental bodies—from courts to securities commissions—monitor the legality of some corporate operations. Furthermore, in the twentieth century there has been a strong trend in Western countries (with the partial exception of the United States) toward the formation of industrial corporations totally owned or at least controlled by the state, which may finance its investments from public funds. Parliament or the government may appoint such corporations' top executives, and may mandate and direct their industrial policies.[19]

Many large economic units, even when their formally "private" capital base allows them to fend off any effective public control over their investments and industrial strategies, operate in fact as semipublic or quasipublic entities vis-à-vis their employees, and to a lesser extent their customers. This is particularly clear when such units engage (as they often do) in activities that are at best distantly related to their central industrial object. As Bahrdt phrases this point:

There are industrial firms that build houses and flats for their employees or make arrangements whereby they can purchase their own homes. They build public parks, schools, churches, and libraries; they arrange concerts and theater outings; they run adult education courses; they look after the aged, widows, and orphans. In other words, a range of functions originally carried out by institutions public not only in the juridical but also in the sociological sense are undertaken by organizations whose activities are nonpublic.... The "private" sphere of operation of a large firm runs right through the existence of the town where it is located, and brings into being a phenomenon to which one may rightly attach the label of industrial feudalism.[20]

Even more significant effects of this kind derive from the fact that large firms constitute for their employees a "quasipolity"—a constitutional and legal system of their own, effectively preserved from interference and control by properly political, state organs.[21] The administrative and semijudicial decisions of such a system are sometimes negotiated between management and the employees' representatives. Yet their tremendous impact on the existence of the employees (and not merely the occupational aspects of that impact, as Bahrdt reminds us) is not mediated within and through the public realm proper, and takes little cognizance of the employees' rights as citizens. Furthermore, the individual employee normally has very little control even over those people or organizations who supposedly represent him to his employer. Finally, where the treatment of employees (pay, security, working conditions, pension rights, fringe benefits) is comparatively generous, the costs are chiefly borne by the larger public—as consumers or taxpayers.

This last remark points to another, all-important result of the dominance of large firms in advanced industrial economies. The operations of such firms deeply modify the working of the market, since they can establish with one another, with smaller firms, with suppliers, and with consumers relations incompatible with the competitive model. For instance, large corporations can usually finance themselves from profits and can thus escape the control of external capital markets; or if they go to such markets for financing, they find them controlled by a few large, corporate investors rather than by a multitude of small savers and investors. Further, large firms capable of generating demand through new products, advertising, and price strategies effectively invert the "classical sequence" whereby the sovereign consumer generated profit opportunities for firms competing for his preferences.

But the competitive market was not just the only proper market; it was also the economic environment presupposed by the liberal state/society distinction. There were two reasons for this. First, the competitive market was self-equilibrating, and could thus dispense with ad hoc regulation and intervention by the state. Second, the competitive market did not appear to countenance the emergence of power relations between economic actors, and thus seemed to leave the state as the only entity wielding power within and for a given national society. The increasing dominance of large firms maximizing not only their profits but also their control over markets, their own growth, and their power over one another and the larger society contradicts both the above assumptions and sharpens immeasurably that challenge I argued earlier the capitalist mode of production always poses to the state's power.

The control that the large firms exercise over the economic process and hence over the whole societal realm allows them to influence the state itself, to persuade the state at the very least not to "interfere" with their activities, and at best to place some of its faculties of rule at their disposal. In the twentieth century, capitalist business has achieved massive (though not uniform) success with this strategy, and has thoroughly affected the state's activities by magnifying their scope, modifying their forms, and orienting them to interests that would not have been recognized as proper public concerns in the nineteenth century. For instance, with the intent of starting, strengthening, or modernizing units operating in the advanced branches of industry, the state now assigns to firms colossal funds, raised from public revenues, to be deployed according to the logic of profit—still intrinsically a "private" logic, whatever the terms under which the firms operate and the funds are assigned. Moreover, the state's costly effort to enlarge and modernize the public education system, whatever the stated aims behind it, serves the end (not always achieved) of supplying industry with the inputs of trained manpower and sophisticated scientific, technological, and managerial know-how it needs to function and to advance. On the output side, too, the state's interest in "stable growth," "full employment," and so forth commits it to massive expenditures intended to support the demand for industrial products —arguably with inflationary side effects. Recent radical interpretations even view most of the so-called welfare expenditures of the contemporary Western state—expenditures we suggested previously were made as a result of the lower strata's newly acquired political effectiveness—as ways in which the state underwrites (largely at the expense of those lower strata as taxpayers) the tremendous costs of the operations of private corporations.[22]

The German constitutional lawyer Böckenförde argues that by engaging in such activities the Western state has subordinated itself to the economic process. (Note that, not being a Marxist, he does not specify the significance of this phenomenon for *class* relations.)

The fact that the contemporary state has identified itself with the economy results in the fact that to a large degree it operates at the service of the industrial-economic process. The range of the state's economic tasks grows, but so does the feebleness of its capacity for self-determination. It carries out functions of regulation and control, but not in the capacity of a "higher third party" that holds the reins; rather, it simply undertakes functions complementary to the industrial-economic process. It is not the state itself that sets what aspects of the economic process will be promoted and regulated; rather, the state reacts to givens and trends that automatically issue from that process itself. Overall control is not exercised by the state, but rather by the industrial-economic process itself.[23]

In my view it is an exaggeration (though not a wild one) to view the state as only a passive participant in the development we have discussed above. The state does not simply react to impulses originating in its counterpart, whether we call it "the industrial-economic process," with Böckenförde, or Capital, or something else. Some encroachments on the state/society line result not from the state's being "pulled" over the line, as it were, but from its "pushing" itself over it. What makes the trend toward the obliteration of the state/society line so powerful is precisely the fact that several phenomena, distinctive and even otherwise mutually contradictory, are at one in causing it.

We have already seen, for instance, how the peculiarly political dynamic of "ins" versus "outs" favored the extension of the franchise and consequently the activation of state policy to the advantage of ever-lower societal strata. But other phenomena discussed in this chapter can be connected with the state's pursuit of its distinctive interests. Take the theme (quintessentially political, in Carl Schmitt's view) of each state's commitment to preserve and aggrandize its own power among states. Clearly under modern conditions this commitment requires a state to give itself an adequate industrial base. But in the advanced industrial era, creating and maintaining such a base requires financial, technological, entrepreneurial, and organizational resources that only the biggest corporations *or* the state can command.[24] And since the biggest corporations are multinational, and as such very awkward customers for a given state,[25*] it often falls to the state alone to take the lead in sponsoring the formation of adequately large and powerful productive undertakings. It is significant that Germany and Japan, which initiated two of the more successful nonliberal variants of capitalist industrialization, were also countries with strong military-political traditions and penchants for aggressiveness—very Schmitt-minded countries, as it were. And French *dirigisme* showed significant advances under DeGaulle—of the Western statesmen of his day probably the most single-mindedly committed to the specificity and the supremacy of "the political."

Böckenförde may be justified in arguing that the state (at any rate in the West) subordinates itself to the apolitical logic of "the industrial-economic process" by becoming overinvolved in economic tasks. But sometimes it gets itself into that predicament while pursuing interests of a noneconomic nature. Indeed, it could avoid the problem only by leaving the country industrially underdeveloped or by surrendering its industrial development to one or more multinational corporations; and both solutions would threaten the country's independent political existence.

The Search for Legitimacy

In the last chapter I followed Max Weber in suggesting that the modern state's specific form of legitimacy is its appeal that its commands be recognized as binding because *legal*, that is, because issued in conformity with properly enacted, general rules. However, I have also followed Carl Schmitt to the extent of recognizing that the motivating force of such a notion is relatively weak because it does not evoke a strong substantive ideal, a universally shared standard of intrinsic validity, but instead refers to purely formal, contentless considerations of procedural correctness. This inherent weakness in its legitimacy becomes a progressively greater liability for the modern state in the postliberal era—on two counts. First, as we shall see below, some institutional premises and expressions of legal rationality became eroded (e.g., the centrality of parliament, the supremacy and generality of law, the division of powers). Second, some developments displacing the state/society line increase the political leverage of social forces (from the underprivileged strata to the new, corporate aggregations of socioeconomic power) that do not stand to gain from the strict observance of procedural rules, and that would prefer, given the chance, to take liberties with the rule of law.

Thus on the one hand, the legitimizing significance of legal rationality remains weak or becomes weaker, whereas on the other hand, industrial advances and the increasing complexity of society (to mention only two factors) make more and more extensive and burdensome that "web of rules" either directly produced by the state or ultimately sanctioned by it, and enveloping social life in all its aspects.[26] Hence it becomes urgent for the state to find a means of renewing its lease on legitimacy, of generating a new legitimizing formula for itself.

Toward the end of the liberal era (late nineteenth and early twentieth centuries), when class contrasts were relatively strong and threatening, most Western states shored up their legitimacy by focusing on imperial and colonial gains and the related international conflicts. Since the Second World War, however, Western nations have ceased to play power politics with one another with the same urgency and visibility as before; they have formed a bloc under the military and diplomatic leadership of the United States, and they have created Atlantic and European alliances and supranational organizations. In an early phase, of course, this mutual accommodation was accompanied by "Cold War" tensions with the Eastern bloc that to some extent replicated—with the addition of new ideological tones—former emphases on national interest. But in the long run, the state found a new and different response to the legitimacy problem: increasingly it treated industrial growth per se as possessing intrinsic and commanding political significance, as constituting a necessary and sufficient standard of each state's performance, and thus as justifying further displacements of the state/society line.

Particularly in the 1950's and 1960's, an ideal variously termed "industrial development," "economic growth," or "affluence" gained an overwhelming grip on the public imagination. It was unanimously endorsed (at any rate in their rhetoric) by political leaders of all persuasions, who treated it on the one hand as utterly self-justifying, and on the other as validating whatever burdens the state might impose on society. It is probably correct to see in this phenomenon another expression of the tyrannical hold of the capitalist mode of production on contemporary social existence at large. (But since something very similar happened at about the same time in Eastern Europe, perhaps we should speak of the tyranny of industrialism.) Yet as I have suggested, one can also see this phenomenon as "co-determined" by developments in the political sphere: for once the experience of two World Wars and the terrifying prospect of nuclear disaster made the pursuit of old-fashioned power politics among Western states an unacceptably disturbing proposition, the pursuit not of power abroad but of prosperity at home became the chief justification for the state's existence and the lodestar of its operations (at least outwardly).

Thus, Böckenförde may be right in arguing that by becoming overinvolved in the industrial-economic process the state subordinates itself to the logic of that process; yet the state's very involvement may be seen as an attempted response to specifically political problems concerning its legitimacy. In fact, it has been argued by A. Gehlen[27] that the developments under discussion add to Max Weber's three types of legitimacy a fourth, contemporary one labeled "social eudaemonic" and characteristic of states seeking legitimacy through acts of rule that assist the economic system in producing an ever-increasing flow of goods and services for the consumer. Note how directly this understanding of legitimacy points to our main theme: as what were originally "private" concerns of individual consumers become of direct and critical "public" significance, the state/society line is obliterated.

Internal Pressures Toward the Expansion of Rule

We must also consider how the very nature and internal constitution of the modern state "push" it over into what in liberal terms was societal territory.

As with any other aspect of the social division of labor, the formation of a specialized political organization generates a set of distinctive, self-regarding interests competing with other parts of the division of labor to maximize its own returns from the working of the whole. In the liberal view, the formation of excessive imbalances in the resulting distribution of facilities and rewards is limited in three ways: by supply-and-demand mechanisms (essentially, by customers taking their demand elsewhere when threatened with exploitation by any one supplier); by diffuse feelings of solidarity overriding invidious interests; and by legal arrangements preventing the component parts of the division of labor from getting away with too much in their dealings with one another and with the whole.

But the very nature of the modern state undercuts the effectiveness of these restraints when applied to *its own* relations to the other parts of the social division of labor. The state monopolizes a crucial faculty—society-wide, generalized coercive power—and to that extent is exempt from supply-and-demand, marketlike curbs. It operates as *itself* the chief referent of feelings of interindividual, intergroup solidarity,[28] and treats submission to itself as the standard expression of those feelings. Finally, the state itself produces and enforces law, the main institutional guarantee of solidarity. In sum, the state is constituted to exercise *rule over society*—whether on behalf of all or part of the society. Hence the state tends to increase its power by widening the scope of its activities, by extending the range of societal interests on which rule is brought to bear.[29]

Under liberalism, three overlapping constitutional arrangements were expected to safeguard the distinctiveness and autonomy of the societal realm in the face of the state: first, the division of powers, whereby the state's power was disaggregated into separate packages of interlocking but mutually limiting faculties of rule entrusted to different organs; second, the liberal "public realm," through which the society itself was supposed to mandate and monitor the exercise of state power; and third, the state's submission to its own law. The erosion and breakdown of the liberal design has resulted mainly from inadequacies in the last two arrangements. As I pointed out in the last chapter, the state could not ultimately be bound by its own law precisely because it was its *own* law, positive law, and as such intrinsically changeable, with only procedural, formal constraints on its changeability. Furthermore, "the" society was in fact inherently fissured by conflicts; and there would always be parties to such conflicts in whose immediate interest it lay to favor and invoke, rather than oppose, some extension of rule into new societal domains. Once these two factors made it juridically and politically possible for the state as a whole to transgress and push back its boundary with society, society could not be adequately safeguarded by the one remaining constitutional arrangement—the division of powers. For what is the use of carefully distributing powers of rule among state organs so that they may "check and balance" one another if those organs can increase their prerogative at the expense of society rather than directly of one another?

Far from helping contain the state within its boundaries, the division of powers in fact led the state as a whole to increase its prerogative through the competition engendered among all its units and subunits over *their* respective prerogatives. For however much the articulation of the system of rule into organs, branches, departments, sections, and so forth may have been conceived as part of a unitary, harmonious organizational design, the component elements in that design became fairly quickly the seats of invidious interests all struggling to increase their autonomy, their reciprocal standing, and their command over resources. And this struggle placed a premium on a unit's ability to define a new societal interest as the legitimate target of its activity, and thus as the justification for its existence and for its standing relative to other units. Furthermore, the individuals elected or appointed to state office cannot be expected to act exclusively on behalf of the interests constitutionally assigned to each office; nor for that matter, can they be expected to act exclusively on behalf of the constitutionally doubtful but compelling micropolitical interests they acquire in the autonomy and standing of the unit of which their office is part. Instead, all individuals orient at least part of their conduct to strictly private interests, particularly to increasing income and status from office-holding, to making a career of it.

Now these individual interests do not so much exercise a direct pressure on the state/society line as add urgency to those interests that do. For instance, a claim that a new phase or aspect of societal business ought to be "administered" by a unit of the civil service can often be used to argue for an increase in the unit's staff. In turn, such an increase may generate new openings at supervisory levels, and thus favor the career interests of the civil servants making up the unit. Under such conditions the force of private interests may be expected to help propel a claim toward realization.

One need not subscribe to popular demonology about "power-grasping bureaucrats" or share the related "metaphysical pathos" to recognize that pressures on the state/society line do originate in these ways (often, of course, in association with pressures from the societal side) and are particularly intense within the state's administrative apparatus.[30] Let us consider soberly the following five statements.

1. Examination of the workings of state organs in the light of economic theory indicates that such organs tend to maximize their budgets rather than the ratio of units of service to units of expended resources.[31] Ultimately, this means that they seek to command ever-increasing amounts of societal resources.

2. The very size and complexity of the administrative apparatus of a contemporary state tend to isolate it (or individual parts of it) from direct societal counterpressures, thus breaking the cybernetic cycle between the administration and the societal environment.[32]

3. Public agencies often reach out into the society and either incorporate sections of it into themselves or make sections of it into the objects of acts of rule; they do this in order to reduce the complexity and turbulence of the societal environment, to stabilize it and their relations to it. It is more comfortable and "natural" for an agency to adopt a posture of administrative control over a given societal interest than to treat it as an autonomous entity or as a party in bargaining relations.

4. Within highly professionalized public agencies, selective recruitment, intense socialization of entrants, strong esprit de corps,

and a shared and valued administrative philosophy of long standing and great prestige can preserve institutional traditions from outside influences. But some such traditions may be preliberal in origin and antiliberal in inspiration; if so, they necessarily impart to the agency's policies a bias against respecting the state/society line. If the "despotic" traditions of some senior sections of the French bureaucracy survived the Revolution itself (as Tocqueville held), they are likely to be still active, in however muted a fashion, under the Fifth Republic. And the Prussian administrative legacy inherited by the Wilhelmine *Obrigkeitsstaat*—and whose hold on the German civil service Weimar could not break and Hitler put to good use—is probably still alive and well in Bonn (and East Berlin!).[33] Finally, Bourbon tendencies—in truth, more favorable to bureaucratic parasitism and corruption than to aggressive encroachment on the autonomy of society—are still powerfully at work within the Italian bureaucracy.

5. Finally, two critical, novel experiences of the twentieth-century state—total war and total dictatorship—have left upon the official mind the world over an indelible and possibly tempting memory of how rapidly, ruthlessly, and efficiently (and with what good conscience) the state can increase its grip on society.

Consequences of the Pressures from State and Society

So far I have suggested some major causes and manifestations—on both sides—of the progressive displacement of the state/society divide in the twentieth century. In this section I shall consider some of the consequences for the structure of the contemporary Western state. The most visible ones are probably the quantitative ones: for example, large increases in the number of public employees and in the share of the social product the state controls through acts of rule and absorbs in its operations; or the proliferation of administrative agencies. I prefer to deal briefly with some qualitative changes, affecting in particular parliamentary institutions and the electoral and legislative processes. Considerable as they are, such changes frequently are not clearly registered in the state's *formal* constitutional structures, which remain those designed between the late eighteenth and the early twentieth centuries.

As we saw in the last chapter, parliament necessarily held a key position in the nineteenth-century state, under whatever name and organizational form it took. Whether or not it was formally the seat of sovereignty, and whatever its relations to the executive, parliament bore the responsibility for processing the political demands expressed through the electoral system into laws—that is, into the essential language and medium of all state operations. Now practically all phenomena displacing the state/society line impinge on this unique position of parliament. In particular, the progressive extension of the franchise not only allows interests not easily "balanceable" with those of the capital-owning class to set the themes of the electoral and legislative processes but also modifies the modalities of those processes.

Previously, contrasts between "balanceable" interests could be settled by open-ended debate between currents of parliamentary opinion,[34] each seeking to increase its support from among a majority of relatively uncommitted parliament members. According to liberal theory (and to a lesser extent practice) each member was accountable to the nation as a whole, not to his own immediate electorate. The latter, being anonymous and unincorporated, could not closely mandate and monitor the members' parliamentary activity (at any rate between elections); it was supposed to trust his judgment, as formed and expressed in parliamentary debate, rather than expect him to abide by a preestablished, narrow program. This diminished the elected member's accountability to and dependence on specific societal interests, and correspondingly increased the leeway for controversy and compromise in the legislative chamber(s). Thus parliament functioned "creatively" (because open-endedly) and produced political and legislative decisions that were not preprogrammed. Of course, extensive and fairly stable alignments among members of parliament existed on both sides of the government/opposition divide. But these alignments were largely internal to parliament itself and were focused not on narrow, contrasting societal interests but on specifically political themes and broad philosophies of state action.

However, as ever-broader masses of the population became enfranchised, only organized parties could effectively mobilize this new, vast, and untrained electorate. But the membership and electoral following of such parties matched the map of societal cleavages more closely than liberal theory deemed decent; and the specific interests those parties represented were not so easily "balanced" against the established ones. Furthermore, because they were organized, parties were able to direct and monitor the conduct of their parliament members fairly closely. In the chamber(s), the party members formed themselves into the "party-in-parliament," with a division of labor and a hierarchical structure, thereby stabilizing majority and minority alignments to an extent previously unknown.

Since the organized parties select the candidates they place on the ballot, and mandate and control their actions when elected, it might seem at first sight that this gives the rank-and-file party members considerable political leverage, thus diffusing political awareness and effectiveness within the population (at whatever cost to the liberal theory of representation). However, whatever the internal constitutions of the parties themselves, their organizational dynamics progressively curb the effective leverage of the rank and file and magnify that of the party leadership.[35] The latter, since the parties themselves are mostly "private" associations, are not accountable to the broad public; and their organizational control over the party makes them increasingly independent even of its membership and electorate.

It is true that most party leaders are also among the party's members of parliament, and in this capacity receive a public investiture. But increasingly the conferral of a public position can be manipulated through internal party arrangements, for the electorate of any given party is largely a "captive" one. Furthermore, since conflicts frequently arise between the party organization and the party-in-parliament, the former elaborates relatively specific ideo-logical guidelines and legislative platforms that it seeks to make binding on the latter.

The open-endedness and creativity of the parliamentary process is thus diminished. Increasingly, parliament is reduced to a highly visible stage on which are enacted vocal, ritualized confrontations between preformed, hierarchically controlled, ideologically char-acterized alignments. Each party-in-parliament may well be rent by internal controversy and engaged in a tug-of-war with its party organization, but in parliament it generally presents a united front, supporting unanimously whatever position is laid down by the leadership as party policy on a given issue. Under such conditions, parliament no longer performs a critical, autonomous role as a mediator between societal interests; instead, its composition and operations simply register the distribution of preferences within the electorate and determine in turn which party will lead the executive. How a party's parliament members will vote on a given issue is decided by the issue's ideological color and by its bearing on the all-important question of whether the party will remain in power or in the opposition. In comparison with these two deter-minants, the *merits* of the issue are relatively insignificant and are not effectively weighed in debate.

Around the middle of the twentieth century, as we have seen, the political process in Western countries begins to revolve around the question of how to promote "industrial development," "affluence," and so forth—this being seen as the only large issue (other than war, hot or cold) that might provide the basis for a reconciliation of societal interests long perceived as "unbalanceable." This de-velopment (besides having direct effects on the state/society line, as already indicated) diminishes the relevance of the parties' ideo-logical heritage, since the issue in question—how to increase the national product—is said to be ultimately a "technical" rather than a political one. The consequent loosening of the party's ideological moorings further increases the autonomy of its leadership with respect to its organizational and electoral base; but it does nothing at all to restore the significance of the electoral process and of parliament.

Elections, fought between increasingly catchall parties, are basically intended to produce a plebiscitary mandate for one party; once secure in its parliamentary majority, that party can then pragmatically develop its policies while obeying a dwindling minimum of doctrinal commitments.[36] Campaigns thus become largely investiture rituals, and are increasingly characterized by marketing techniques, with a great deal of image-mongering and pseudopersonalization of issues through a focus on candidate "charisma." In elaborating or justifying their policies between elections, both the party (or coalition of parties) in power and its opponents appeal less and less to ideological criteria (often sneeringly characterized as "party-political") and more and more to the reasonings of "experts" in macroeconomic and administrative management. This is only appropriate, because the whole society is increasingly conceived of as a firm intent on maximizing or optimizing the ratio of its outputs to its inputs. Accordingly, the state's task is seen as that of managing that firm after the fashion of the contemporary large corporation—with a "technostructure" erecting and operating multiple overlapping "sociotechnical" systems.

Once the political process is so (mis)conceived, parliament has little of distinctive significance to contribute to it. The vacuum left by the devaluation of ideology (or at any rate of certain ideologies) is filled not by a renewal of open-ended discourse but by an appeal to economic, technological, and managerial "expertise." And to supply that expertise or to control its employment in the conduct of rule does not seem a job parliament can adequately do. Instead, the job falls mainly to the professional civil service, which enlists the support of research institutes, planning units, and consultative bodies manned chiefly by the "scientific estate" and by spokesmen for the larger corporations and other interest groups. As a result, administrative decisions are increasingly articulated in a language that effectively screens them from parliamentary criticism and public debate, and that frequently provides a convenient cover for the interests actually dictating those decisions. The classical parliamentary means for monitoring and auditing the operations of the executive (from the vote on the budget to parliamentary questions) lose effectiveness in the face of this phenomenon and related ones. For instance, many new administrative agencies arise outside the framework of ministerial organization and even in formal terms are not easily held accountable to parliament through its right to question ministers. Paradoxically, the gigantic growth of public revenues and expenditures makes parliamentary control more necessary than ever but also increasingly impossible; the bewildering size and complexity of budgets and other accounting instruments both demand and prohibit parliamentary oversight. Moreover, the legislative overload straining the working capacity of most parliaments reduces the amount of time available for monitoring activities.

These last points should not suggest that parliaments can effectively defend their much-threatened supremacy over the executive and the administration through their legislative prerogative. Executive and administration in fact largely control the volume and the content of the legislation they themselves process through parliament. In the eyes of ministers and top civil servants, legislation has become too important to be left to legislators. Laws are drafted almost exclusively outside parliament; they deal largely with matters of primarily administrative significance; and they mostly serve to validate in formal terms decisions reached by civil servants in their technocratic wisdom (much assisted by interested pressure groups). Furthermore, contemporary legislation has largely lost those features of generality and abstractness that made "classical" legislation into the instrument par excellence of parliamentary supremacy. Many laws are effectively ad hoc measures of an intrinsically administrative nature given the form of law in order to legalize the expenditures they involve and shield ministers and civil servants from having to take political or personal responsibility for them. In view of the enormous tasks of "societal management" borne by contemporary governments, administrative action cannot be meaningfully programmed in the classical manner—that is, by means of a law stating general conditions under which a given administrative action is to be taken. Instead, programs directing an agency, say, to increase the country's steel-making capacity by x percent, or to reduce industrial pollution in a given river by y percent over z years, must leave the measures to be taken toward the target in question to administrative discretion, supposedly informed by the appropriate nonlegal expertise.[37] It then becomes impossible for parliament (or a judicial organ, or for that matter a higher agency)[38] to control the agency's conduct by checking whether it corresponds with abstractly stated rules, since no such rules do or can exist.

The cumulative impact of all these phenomena—to which one might add such others as the operations of multinational firms and supranational organizations—is to shunt parliament away from the effective center of a country's political life, leaving in control the state's executive organs, and especially its administrative apparatus, now thoroughly "interlaced" with those various controlling nonstate forces. Yet parliament remains the chief institutional link between the citizenry and the state. If it ceases to operate as an *effective* link, what or who can politically direct, control, and moderate the ever-growing mutual involvement between state and society?

The parties demand from the electorate a more and more generic, less and less binding mandate; yet they cannot effectively be held accountable for its execution, since whatever their differences on other issues they all cherish their shared monopoly of institutionalized political representation. The very size and complexity of the administrative apparatus insulates it from political control. The so-called media are no longer relatively open channels for political expression and forums for public debate (as newspapers originally were). In several Western countries in the 1960's and 1970's the courts have enjoyed occasional successes in reasserting much-battered ideas of legality in the conduct of public business; but theirs is a rearguard action, limited in its scope by its primary reference to criminal laws. Nor is it plausible to expect an effective defense of the distinctiveness and autonomy of the societal realm to be mounted by economic and other organizations; on the contrary, most of them appear only too eager to "colonize" the political realm, overtly or covertly appropriating public resources and usurping faculties of rule in order to place them at the service of sectional social interests (at best) or of the narrow oligarchies that run them (at worst).

These considerations, purposely overstated, point to what seem to have become structural givens of the political process and its relations to the wider society in the contemporary West. Their implications become even more ominous when one considers also a few conjunctural facts concerning the countries in question in the period between the mid-1960's and the mid-1970's. The general import of these facts is that the institutional apparatus of the state, even apart from the question of whether it does or does not respect its original constitutional design and thus its boundary with society, has serious difficulties with a number of threatening problems. These problems are interconnected, and they are also linked with the phenomena discussed in the previous sections. Here, however, I shall disregard the connections and simply list the problems alone.

1. Political dissent over the period mentioned manifests itself frequently in unconstitutional and sometimes in criminal forms; and its aims are sometimes the total rejection and subversion of, or secession from, the established political system. At least in some cases, these developments are the result of the closing off of constitutional means of political expression to the broad public, which makes the system impenetrable by and unresponsive to legitimate demands. Furthermore, the reactions of established authorities often violate constitutional principles in turn, thereby increasing the political alienation of certain social groups.

2. The so-called "welfare system" of various states appears both unable to remedy any but the most extreme forms of economic and social deprivation and incapable of effectively reducing the range

of wider socioeconomic inequalities; moreover, its direct and administrative costs place an increasingly burdensome fiscal strain on the population and the productive system.

3. Drastic and repeated failures of statesmanship and of political judgment, as well as glaring "scandals" and "affairs," reveal that at the very top of some states the intellectual and moral qualities of political leadership are demoralizingly low.

4. The state's law enforcement apparatus proves increasingly incapable of guaranteeing the citizens' security in public places and in their homes, the wholesomeness and amenity of their physical environment, and the prevention and repression of large-scale depredations of the public (both as consumers and as taxpayers) by business firms.

5. Generally, the administrative apparatus of most states, though absorbing an increasing share of the national product, displays a decreasing capacity for effective societal management.

6. Most importantly, the state machinery for monitoring, supporting, and steering the national economy proves inadequate to its tasks time and again. By the mid-1970's in most Western countries, the Keynesian and post-Keynesian apparatus of economic policy is in disarray in the face of a baffling combination of stubborn inflationary and recessionary trends.

This last phenomenon (whatever its causes) is politically significant especially insofar as it affects the state's legitimacy. I have previously suggested that legal-rational legitimacy is inherently weak as a source of moral motivations for compliance, that it has been further weakened by developments discussed in this chapter, that in the 1950's and 1960's all Western states sought to counter the resulting legitimacy deficit by claiming that rule was exercised chiefly in order to sustain industrial development, and so forth. But in the 1960's some sizable minorities began to question the moral significance of what seemed to be the continuous advance of Western populations toward a better standard of living and the moral validity of the claim for loyal compliance the state was basing on that advance. In the 1970's, as we have seen, that advance has become more laborious and uncertain; its benefits have been revealed to be much more unequally distributed than had seemed to be the case; and in some states, at least, it appears to have been interrupted altogether, perhaps for good. Thus the legitimacy formula in question (like any other such formula in a comparable situation) threatens to "go into reverse," to increase rather than fill the legitimacy vacuum.

Viewed from the standpoint of the state, this phenomenon opens three main possibilities. First, the state can try to do without a legitimizing formula and rely on intimidating and repressing the disaffected sections of the citizenry and on favoring the rest in order to maintain control over society. Second, it can fall back on the earlier legitimizing formula of power politics, seeking to generate a wider consensus by pointing to the real or imaginary military threat posed to one state or coalition of states by other states or coalitions. Or, third, it can try to "sell" the society on a new formula—preferably one superficially attractive enough to evoke wide acclaim (with the help of the media), and general enough not to commit the state to anything in particular. (In the early 1970's "The Quality of Life" appeared to be a plausible candidate for such a formula.)

Whatever their respective probabilities of success, none of these outcomes (or even possible combinations of them) appears attractive. All seek to carry forward the basic trend in the institutional development of the modern state—the gathering unto it of ever more extensive and formidable faculties and facilities of rule—despite awareness that, paradoxically, that trend is making the state increasingly incapable of effectively exercising rule, of establishing rational control over the social process. Furthermore, all these outcomes more or less openly forsake two political ideas that, though they have sustained the basic trend in the state's development over the last two centuries, have at the same time afforded it a justification and a corrective: the liberal idea of the rule of law, and the democratic idea of the participation of the ruled in the process of rule. Only these two ideas connect the past evolution of the modern state with the moral heritage of the West, and thus with a wider ethical vision of humanity as the collective protagonist of a universal moral venture.[39]

Personally, I think that in seeking both moral inspiration and strategic guidance, Western opposition to the present disturbing tendencies in state/society relations must turn once more to those (and perhaps to some other) liberal and democratic ideas.[40] I am aware that on a number of grounds this sounds like a counsel of despair. Both liberalism and democracy have been tried and found wanting, it might be argued, or indeed have been so much a part of the problem in the past that we cannot seriously consider them now a part of the solution. One may also point to inherent and possibly insoluble contrasts between liberalism and democracy, and doubt the possibility of institutionally embodying both except at the cost of compromises that would weaken and disfigure each. Or one may suggest, more hopefully, that socialism is an alternative that transcends both liberalism and democracy by forcefully raising the problems set by the economic structure of society.

Yet in my view socialism is less relevant than liberalism and democracy to the dilemmas that face contemporary Western society as a result of trends in the state's structure and functioning. Liberalism and democracy have the advantage over socialism of directly addressing some key problems arising from the necessity of rule instead of downgrading such problems to the status of technical matters to be settled unproblematically after a revolution in the control over the means of production.[41] To those problems liberalism and democracy may perhaps (on the present record) offer wrong solutions; but wrong solutions to the right problems may be more valuable, theoretically and pragmatically, than a misguided attempt to ignore or bypass those problems.

Thus, insofar as the range of sources of inspiration available in Western societies today is still bounded by liberalism, democracy, and socialism (with their several variants)—and I for one cannot look beyond those bounds[42]—an imaginative and innovative reconsideration of the traditions of liberalism and democracy appears as a necessary, though of course not sufficient, condition for positive action.

Notes

Notes

PREFACE

1. See my review article "Political Sociology," *Cambridge Review*, 9 (1973), pp. 33–37.

2. See A. Giddens, *Politics and Sociology in the Thought of Max Weber* (London, 1972), and D. Bentham, *Max Weber and the Theory of Modern Politics* (London, 1974).

3. For a review of some lines of current Marx-inspired work on the state, see J. Esser, *Einführung in die materialistische Staatstheorie* (Frankfurt, 1975). I have given a very compact account of Marx's own views on the state in *Images of Society: Essays on the Sociological Theories of Tocqueville, Marx, and Durkheim* (Stanford, Calif., 1972), pp. 139–43.

4. See, for instance, K. Marx and F. Engels, *Staatstheorie: Materialien zur Rekonstruktion der marxistischen Staatstheorie* (Frankfurt, 1974).

5. For a survey of these developments, see A. Passerin d'Entrèves, *The Modern Notion of the State* (Oxford, 1965).

6. On the interaction between political thought and political practice in general, see R. M. Unger, *Knowledge and Politics* (New York, 1975); for the specific impact of that interaction on state-building, see N. Matteucci, *Organizzazione del potere e libertà* (Turin, 1976).

7. "Modern" is in a sense superfluous, since the very notion of the state involves those characteristics (notably the intensification, continuity, and accentuated institutionalization of rule) that governance over larger populations acquired for the first time in the *modern* West. For a philological argument to this effect, based on a detailed reconstruction of the origins of the term "state" in various European lan-

guages, see W. Mager, *Zur Entstehung des modernen Staatsbegriffes* (Wiesbaden, 1968).

CHAPTER I

1. The interested reader may wish to complement my choice by considering such contemporary treatments of the nature of politics as J. Freund, *L'Essence du politique* (Paris, 1965); B. de Jouvenel, *The Pure Theory of Politics* (Cambridge, Eng., 1963); J. Y. Calvez, *Introduction à la vie politique* (Paris, 1970); and H. P. Platz, *Vom Wesen der politischen Macht* (Bonn, 1971).

2. D. Easton, *The Political System* (New York, 1953), chap. 5.

3. See M. S. Olmstead, *The Small Group* (New York, 1959), pp. 62ff.

4. E. Durkheim, *De la division du travail social* (9th ed.; Paris, 1967), Book I, chap. 7.

5. A recent edition of this text is C. Schmitt, *Der Begriff des politischen* (Berlin, 1963). A brief passage from this work is translated in S. N. Eisenstadt, ed., *Political Sociology* (New York, 1971), pp. 459–60.

6. The significance of "otherdom" is also emphasized by Jouvenel and, following him, by Calvez in the works cited in note 1 above.

7. See, for example, H. Ryffel, *Grundprobleme der Rechts- und Staats-philosophie* (Neuwied, 1969), pp. 228ff, 371ff.

8. An interesting discussion in English of Schmitt's ideas—G. Schwab, *The Challenge of the Exception* (Berlin, 1970)—is focused on the relationship between emergency and routine in political activity.

9. Schmitt, pp. 33, 34, 37.

10. *Ibid.*, pp. 49f.

11. Here I follow G. Ritter, *Die Dämonie der Macht* (Munich, 1948).

12. G. E. C. Catlin, *Science and Method of Politics* (New York, 1927), p. 262.

13. See K. Löwith, *Gesammelte Abhandlungen* (Stuttgart, 1960), pp. 93ff.

14. Quoted in the *Times Higher Education Supplement*, August 27, 1976, p. 13.

15. The most influential and explicit proponents of this theoretical approach among the classic sociologists are probably Spencer and Durkheim. (The contribution of Simmel is for some reason less frequently noted.) Notable among contemporary statements are T. Parsons, *Societies* and *The System of Modern Societies* (Englewood Cliffs, N.J., 1966 and 1971); N. Smelser, *Essays in Sociological Explanation* (Englewood Cliffs, N.J., 1968), Part II; and N. Luhmann, "System-

theoretische Argumentationen," in J. Habermas and N. Luhmann, *Theorie der Gesellschaft oder Sozialtechnologie* (Frankfurt, 1971), esp. pp. 361ff.

16. See the sharp critique of old and new forms of "social evolutionism" in B. Giesen and M. Schmid, "System und Evolution," *Soziale Welt*, 26 (1975):385ff.

17. See M. I. Finley, *Democracy Ancient and Modern* (London, 1973).

18. See the opening pages of L. Ranke, *The History of the Popes* (London, 1847), vol. 1, pp. 1–6; also F. Ruffini, *Relazioni tra stato e chiesa* (Bologna, 1976).

19. See O. Brunner, "Freiheitsrechte in der altständischen Gesellschaft," in E.-W. Böckenförde, ed., *Staat und Gesellschaft* (Darmstadt, 1976), p. 30.

CHAPTER II

1. For example, P. Anderson's impressive and valuable books, *Passages from Antiquity to Feudalism* and *Lineages of the Absolutist State* (London, 1975), though employing (among others) some secondary sources used in this work, do not acknowledge the Ständestaat to have been as distinctive as I believe was the case. And not all German works follow the typology I use, either; see, for instance, H. Mitteis, *The State in the Middle Ages: A Comparative Constitutional History of Feudal Europe* (Amsterdam, 1975). On the other hand, for an important statement of the importance of the Ständestaat by a British historian, see A. R. Myers, "The Parliaments of Europe and the Age of the Estates," *History*, 61 (1975):11–26.

2. The most significant precedent is, of course, M. Weber, *Economy and Society* (Totowa, N.J., 1968), vol. 3, pp. 1075–1111; but see also, among his contemporaries, F. Oppenheimer, *System der Soziologie*, vol. 2 (*Der Staat*), (2d ed.; Stuttgart, 1964), sec. 5. Among contemporary treatments, see R. Bendix, *Nation-Building and Citizenship* (New York, 1964), chap. 2; and, more recently, R. M. Unger, *Law in Modern Society* (New York, 1976), chap. 3. See also my *Images of Society: Essays on the Sociological Theories of Tocqueville, Marx, and Durkheim* (Stanford, Calif., 1972), sec. 1.

3. For the wider meaning, see P. Goubert, *L'Ancien Régime* (Paris, 1969), vol. 1.

4. One of the more useful aspects of P. Anderson's two books cited in note 1 above is the sustained attention to the "national" variants of the processes they analyze.

5. For what is still a most valuable discussion of the environment in which feudalism arose, see M. Bloch, *Feudal Society* (London, 1961), vol. 1, parts 1 and 2.

6. See R. E. Sullivan, ed., *The Coronation of Charlemagne: What Did It Signify?* (New York, 1972).

7. See W. Schlesinger, "Lord and Follower in Germanic Institutional History," in F. Cheyette, ed., *Lordship and Community in Medieval Europe* (New York, 1968), pp. 64–99.

8. See R. Boutruche, *Seigneurie et féodalité* (Paris, 1970), vol. 2, book 1, for a general discussion of *seigneurie* in the heyday of feudalism.

9. Cited in M. Pacaut, *Les Structures politiques de l'Occident médiéval* (Paris, 1969), p. 158.

10. See G. Fourquin, *Lordship and Feudalism in the Middle Ages* (London, 1976), parts 1 and 2.

11. See T. Mayer, "I fondamenti dello stato moderno tedesco nell'alto medioevo," in E. Rotelli and P. Schiera, eds., *Lo stato moderno. I: Dal medioevo all'età moderna* (Bologna, 1971), pp. 21–50. I speak of an anachronism because Mayer (with other respected students, e.g., H. Mitteis) seems to me to take the wrong side of the protracted dispute over whether one should apply the designation "state" to the feudal system of rule. For a sketchy review of this dispute, see the Introduction to H. H. Hofmann, ed., *Die Entstehung des modernen souveränen Staates* (Cologne, 1967).

12. G. Duby, *La Société aux XIe et XIIe siècles dans la region mâconnaise* (Paris, 1953).

13. *Ibid.*, pp. 170–71.

14. Cited in Boutruche, vol. 2, p. 418.

15. Mitteis rightly emphasizes the political significance of whether or not the overlord (particularly the territorial ruler) managed to establish a direct relationship with the lower vassals. For a general, juridically oriented discussion of the feudal relationship, see H. Ganshof, *Feudalism* (3d ed.; London, 1964).

16. See H. Goez, *Der Leihezwang* (Tübingen, 1962), which examines the significance of the "compulsion to grant" in the context of the relations between king and higher feudatories.

17. Cited in Pacaut, p. 162.

18. For a succinct yet solidly grounded and impressive analysis of this process, see J. Dhondt, *L'alto medioevo* (Milan, 1970).

19. See especially O. Brunner, *Land und Herrschaft* (4th ed.; Vienna, 1959), pp. 1–110.

20. Cited in Dhondt, pp. 284–85.

21. Boutruche, vol. 1, pp. 230–33, emphasizes this point, which is in any case a charge of long standing against the political entropy of the feudal system.

22. German terminology associates this depersonalization with not "objectification" (*Versachlichung*) but "reification" (*Verdinglichung*) of the feudal relation. See this formulation in O. Hintze, "Wesen und Verbreitung des Feudalismus," in O. Hintze, *Feudalismus-Kapitalismus* (Göttingen, 1970), p. 15, and in H. Mitteis, *Der Staat des hohen Mittelalters* (7th ed.; Weimar, 1962), p. 4. The latter passage is not in the English translation of Mitteis's work cited in note 1.

23. On this point, see J. R. Strayer, *On the Medieval Origins of the Modern State* (Princeton, N.J., 1970).

24. See O. Brunner, *Adeliges Landleben und europäischer Geist* (Salzburg, 1949), chaps. 1, 2; N. Elias, *Über den Prozess der Zivilisation* (2d ed.; Bern, 1969), vol. 1. I have made no reference in the text to the institution of chivalry, which has considerable significance in this context. See, for instance, the sections on "The Growth of the Noble Class" and "The Aristocratic Mind" in Cheyette, ed.

25. This point is emphasized in the opening pages of Brunner, *Adeliges Landleben*.

26. On the significance of the right to resist one's superior, see F. Kern, *Kingship and Law in the Middle Ages* (Oxford, 1939), part 1.

27. Cited in Boutruche, pp. 416–17.

28. See J. Lemarignier, *La France médiévale: Institutions et société* (Paris, 1971), p. 234.

29. Duby, pp. 549, 553, 557–59, 564–66.

30. I borrow this expression from the chapter title "Transfeudale Kräfte der Hochkulturen," in A. Rüstow, *Ortsbestimmung der Gegenwart* (Bern, 1950), vol. 1, p. 205.

31. See F. L. Carsten, *Princes and Parliaments in Germany* (Oxford, 1959), pp. 426f.

CHAPTER III

1. See, for instance, W. Näf, "Frühformen des modernen Staates im Spätmittelalter," in H. H. Hofmann, ed., *Die Entstehung des modernen souveränen Staates* (Cologne, 1967), p. 110.

2. Most of the points made in this section derive from Max Weber's comparative discussion of the Western as against the classical or the oriental city in *Economy and Society* (Totowa, N.J., 1968), vol. 3, chap. 16.

3. J. Dhondt, *L'alto medioevo* (Milan, 1970), pp. 335–36.

4. On the significance of this phenomenon (not only with reference to the rise of the towns), see R. Fossier, *Histoire sociale de l'occident médiéval* (Paris, 1970), pp. 186ff.

5. Cited in J. le Goff, *Il basso medioevo* (Milan, 1967), p. 80.

6. Dhondt, pp. 335–36.

7. J. Dhondt, " 'Ordini' o 'potenze': l'esempio degli Stati di Fiandra," in E. Rotelli and P. Schiera, eds., *Lo stato moderno*, vol. 1 (Bologna, 1971), p. 252.

8. Though political phenomena that can be meaningfully labeled "feudal" have occurred also in civilizations other than the medieval West (see, for instance, R. Boutruche, *Seigneurie et féodalité* [2d ed.; Paris, 1968], vol. 1, book 2, and the bibliography), there appear to have been no systems parallel to the Ständestaat. See M. Weber, *The Protestant Ethic and the Spirit of Capitalism* (London, 1931), p. 16. For a discussion of this thesis, see A. R. Myers, "The Parliaments of Europe and the Age of the Estates," *History*, 61 (1975): 11ff.; and D. G. Gerhardt, "Regionalismus und Ständeswesen als ein Grundthema europäischer Geschichte," in his *Alte und neue Welt in vergleichender Geschichtsbetrachtung* (Göttingen, 1962), chap. 1.

9. T. H. Marshall, "The Nature and Determinants of Social Status," in his *Class, Citizenship and Social Development* (Garden City, N.J., 1965), p. 193.

10. For an admirably comprehensive, typological treatment of the most important variants, see O. Hintze, "Typologie der ständischen Verfassungen des Abendlandes," in his *Feudalismus-Kapitalismus* (Göttingen, 1970), pp. 48–67. An excellent survey is A. Marongiu, *Medieval Parliaments* (London, 1968).

11. L. Febvre, *Philippe II et la Franche-Comté* (2d ed.; Paris, 1970), pp. 47ff. (The first edition of this book was published in 1912.)

12. *Ibid.*

13. *Ibid.*

14. On the relationship between feudal and ständisch assemblies, and on intermediate cases, see T. N. Bisson, *Assemblies and Representation in Languedoc in the Thirteenth Century* (Princeton, N.J., 1964).

15. O. Brunner, in one of the many writings where he develops this view—"Die Freiheitsrechte in der altständischen Gesellschaft," in *Aus Verfassungs- und Landsgeschichte: Festschrift Theodor Mayer* (Thorbecke, 1954), vol. 1, pp. 290 ff—specifically refers to the conceptual argument by Theodor Mayer I quoted in the last chapter. The argument views the feudal state as "an association of persons" and the mature

modern state as an "institutional-territorial" one. See note 10 to Chapter 2 above.

16. The Swiss historian W. Näf has collected and edited numerous historical documents containing "compacts of rule"; for a synthesis of his findings, see his essay cited in note 1 above.

17. Quoted from M. Pacaut, *Les Structures politiques de l'occident médiéval* (Paris, 1969), pp. 391f.

18. On this and other aspects of the Ständestaat as a step in the development of the modern state, see two articles by P. Schiera, "Società per ceti" and "Stato moderno," in N. Bobbio and N. Matteucci, eds., *Dizionario di politica* (Turin, 1976), pp. 961ff, 1,006ff.

19. See P. Schiera, "L'introduzione delle 'Akzise' in Prussia e i suoi riflessi nella dottrina contemporanea," *Annali della Fondazione italiana per la storia amministrativa*, 2 (1965): 287.

20. F. L. Carsten, *Princes and Parliaments in Germany* (Oxford, 1959), pp. 425ff.

21. Näf, p. 112.

22. For a synthesis of such discussions, see Carsten, chap. 6.

23. This Prussian case is recounted in a very instructive way in P. Schiera, "L'introduzione delle 'Akzise' in Prussia."

24. The patrimonial-bureaucratic administrative component of the Ständestaat is emphasized in O. Brunner, "Feudalism: The History of a Concept," in F. Cheyette, ed., *Lordship and Community in Medieval Europe* (New York, 1968), pp. 51–53.

25. See, for example, L. Martines, *Lawyers and Statecraft in Renaissance Florence* (Princeton, N.J., 1963), though it concerns an atypical case—Florence having been a city-state in the period we are considering here. Note, however, that many of the political-administrative devices characteristic of the urban polities were developed for the first time not by and for them, but by and for ecclesiastical, and especially monastic, bodies. See E. Schmitt, *Repräsentation und Revolution* (Munich, 1969), p. 37.

26. This point has been emphasized in H. Spangenberg, *Vom Lehnstaat zum Ständestaat* (Aalen, 1964), chap. 6. (The first edition of this book was published in 1912.)

27. See K. V. Räumer, "Absolute Staat, korporative Libertät, persönliche Freiheit," pp. 173ff in the collection edited by H. H. Hofmann cited in note 1 above.

28. E.-W. Böckenförde, "La pace di Westphalia e il diritto d'alleanza dei ceti dell'Impero," in E. Rotelli and P. Schiera, eds., *Lo stato moderno*, vol. 3 (Bologna, 1974), p. 339.

CHAPTER IV

1. J. Vicens Vives, "La struttura amministrativa statale nei secoli XVI e XVII," in E. Rotelli and P. Schiera, eds., *Lo stato moderno*, vol. 1 (Bologna, 1971), pp. 226f.

2. For this line of interpretation see, for instance, B. de Jouvenel, *On Power* (Boston, 1962).

3. A. Negri, "Problemi di storia dello Stato moderno: Francia, 1610–1650," *Rivista critica di storia della filosofia*, 22 (1967): 195f.

4. Quoted in W. F. Church, *The Impact of Absolutism on France* (New York, 1969), p. 30.

5. See I. Wallerstein, *The Modern World System* (New York, 1974), chap. 3.

6. Though Italian cities are generally atypical, the example of Lucca as examined in M. Berengo, *Nobili e mercanti nella Lucca del Cinquecento* (Turin, 1965), is very instructive, and not particularly atypical. The towns' "military muscle," incidentally, had been fatally weakened by the development of artillery, which made the less sophisticated forms of urban fortification obsolete.

7. G. N. Clark, *The Seventeenth Century* (London, 1927), p. 21.

8. F. Galgano, "La categoria storica del diritto commerciale," in G. Tarello, ed., *Materiali per una storia della cultura giuridica*, vol. 6 (Bologna, 1976), pp. 48ff.

9. This brief account of the urban element's loss of political nerve is largely inspired by Tocqueville's *L'Ancien Régime* (Oxford, 1904).

10. See D. Bitton, *The French Nobility in Crisis 1560–1640* (Stanford, Calif., 1969).

11. See M. Howard, *War in European History* (Oxford, 1976), chaps 2–4.

12. There were other significant implications of a fiscal nature, as I have already suggested in an earlier chapter. See N. Elias, *Über den Prozess der Zivilisation* (2d ed.; Bern, 1969), vol. 2, pp. 279ff.; and A. Rüstow, *Ortsbestimmung der Gegenwart* (Bern, 1950), vol. 1, pp. 239ff.

13. Clark, pp. 86ff. For the examples of Prussia and Austria, see H. O. Meissner, "Das Regierungs- und Behördensystem Maria Theresas und der preussische Staat," in H. Hofmann, ed., *Die Entstehung des modernen souveränen Staates* (Cologne, 1967), pp. 210ff.

14. See the place held by ständisch institutions in the survey of prerevolutionary European constitutional structures in R. R. Palmer, *The Age of the Democratic Revolution* (Princeton, N.J., 1959), vol. 1.

15. One might oppose to this understanding of the monarch's position, of course, the famous saying "l'état, c'est moi," attributed to Louis XIV and often interpreted as asserting a close identification between the state and the physical person of the individual ruler. Judging from recent writing on this question, however, it appears that one may conclude as follows: Louis probably never said it; if he did say it, he did not mean it that way; if he did mean it that way, then he did not know what he was talking about. See F. Hartung, "L'état, c'est moi," in his *Staatsbildende Kräfte der Neuzeit* (Berlin, 1961), pp. 93ff; and E. Schmitt, *Repräsentation und Revolution* (Munich, 1969), pp. 67ff.

16. See the outstanding sociological reconstruction of the court setting and of its political significance in N. Elias, *Die höfische Gesellschaft* (Neuwied, 1969).

17. The unequaled, firsthand source concerning the French absolutist court remains the Duc de Saint-Simon; see L. Norton, trans. and ed., *The Historical Memoirs of the Duc de Saint-Simon* (London, 1970–72), 3 vols.

18. Following N. Elias in *Die höfische Gesellschaft*, W. Lepenies analyzes with great insight some psychological consequences of the constrained position of the court nobles in his *Melancholie und Gesellschaft* (Frankfurt, 1972).

19. On the prototypical arrangement for selecting, empowering, and controlling this kind of officialdom, see O. Hintze, "Der Commissarius und seine geschichtliche Bedeutung für die allgemeine Verwaltungsgeschichte," in his *Staat und Verfassung* (2d ed.; Göttingen, 1962), pp. 264ff.

20. *Ibid.*, p. 275.

21. See O. Brunner, "Vom Gottesgnadentum zum monarchischen Prinzip," in H. Hofmann, ed., pp. 115ff.

22. The best treatment of the "reception," though focused on the German case, is F. Wieacker, *Privatrechtsgeschichte der Neuzeit* (2d ed.; Göttingen, 1967), part 2.

23. See Tocqueville's famous (though sometimes disputed) judgment on the intrinsic authoritarian tendencies of Roman law in his first note to *L'Ancien Régime*, pp. 229–31.

24. See Galgano, "La categoria storica."

25. See H. Rosenberg, *Bureaucracy, Aristocracy and Autocracy* (Cambridge, Mass., 1958); H. Jacoby, *The Bureaucratization of the World* (Berkeley, Calif., 1974), chap. 2.

26. P. Schiera, "L'introduzione delle 'Akzise' in Prussia e i suoi riflessi nella dottrina contemporanea," *Annali della Fondazione italiana per la storia amministrativa*, 2 (1965): 294.

27. Once more, this view is primarily inspired by Tocqueville.

28. See F. Hartung, "Aufgeklärter Absolutismus," in H. Hofmann, ed., pp. 149ff.; and J. Gagliardo, *Enlightened Despotism* (London, 1967).

29. R. Kühnl, *Due forme di dominio borghese: liberalismo e fascismo* (Italian translation of *Formen bürgerlicher Herrschaft*, vol. 1; Milan, 1973), pp. 25f., argues, from a Marxist viewpoint, that absolutism favored the development of capitalism; but he recognizes that some absolutist policies were widely at variance with particular class demands and values of the bourgeoisie. For a sophisticated interpretation of an alternative viewpoint, which also appeals to Marxism but stresses the connections between absolutism and the class/estate interests of the nobility, see P. Anderson, *Lineages of the Absolutist State* (London, 1975), chaps. 1–2. Apparently, from a Marxist viewpoint one can argue either that the monarchy "worked for" the bourgeoisie or that it "worked for" the nobility; what, for some reason or other, appears out of the question is that the monarchy may have "worked for" itself, meaning of course not the monarch and his dynasty alone but the whole apparatus of rule surrounding him.

30. From this point in the chapter, I draw heavily on J. Habermas, *Strukturwandel der Öffentlichkeit* (5th ed.; Neuwied, 1971).

31. R. Koselleck, *Kritik und Krise, Ein Beitrag zur Pathogenese der bürgerlichen Welt* (Freiburg, 1959), is particularly enlightening on the role played by international Freemasonry, which was, in a sense, both a secret and a public institution.

32. On the extent to which in France particularly "the bourgeoisie becomes politicized prior to having a political role to play," see G. Durand, *Etats et institutions: XVIe–XVIIIe siècles* (Paris, 1969), pp. 291ff.

33. Throughout this book I have purposely paid little attention to the concept of the "nation" and to its considerable historical connection with that of the "state." An argument for separating the discussions of these two concepts, and of the attendant historical processes, has recently been put forward by C. Tilly in his introduction to C. Tilly, ed., *The Formation of National States in Western Europe* (Princeton, N.J., 1975). For an introductory discussion of "nation" and "nationalism," see E. Lemberg, *Nationalismus* (Reinbek, 1964), esp. vol. 1, section 2.

CHAPTER V

1. For a sophisticated contemporary treatment of the modern legal system, see R. M. Unger, *Law in Modern Society* (New York, 1976), chap. 2.

2. See H. Jahrreiss's 1957 article, "Die Souveränität des Staates. Ein Wort—mehrere Begriffe—viele Missverständnisse," in H. Hofmann, ed., *Die Entstehung des Modernen Souveränen Staates* (Cologne, 1967), pp. 35ff. (esp. pp. 37–41).

3. See O. Hintze's 1902 article, "The Formation of States and Constitutional Development," in F. Gilbert, trans. and ed., *The Historical Essays of Otto Hintze* (New York, 1975), pp. 158ff. (esp. pp. 164–67).

4. J. Kenyon, in his review of A. Toynbee's *Mankind and Mother Earth: A Narrative History of the World*, in *The Observer*, July 11, 1976, p. 23.

5. The role of the relations between Empire and Papacy in the emergence of the modern states system is particularly emphasized by H. Mitteis in *The State in the Middle Ages* (Amsterdam, 1975).

6. L. Gross, "The Peace of Westphalia: 1648–1948," in R. A. Falk and W. F. Hanrieder, eds., *International Law and Organization: An Introductory Reader* (Philadelphia, 1969), pp. 53–54.

7. The economic components of this phenomenon have been impressively spelled out in I. Wallerstein, *The Modern World System: Capitalist Agriculture and the Origins of the European World Economy in the 16th Century* (San Francisco, 1974).

8. Hintze, "Formation of States."

9. See E. Lemberg, *Nationalismus* (Reinbek, 1964), vol. 1, pp. 102ff.

10. K. Polanyi, *Origins of Our Time: The Great Transformation* (London, 1945), chap. 1.

11. W. Mommsen has reconstructed the role these phenomena played in the evolving political thinking of Max Weber in *Max Weber und die deutsche Politik 1890–1920* (2d ed.; Tübingen, 1974).

12. G. Jellinek, *Allgemeine Staatslehre* (3d ed.; Berlin, 1928), pp. 319f.

13. See, for example, G. Rochat, "L'esercito e il fascismo," in G. Quazza, ed., *Fascismo e società italiana* (Turin, 1973), pp. 89ff. (esp. pp. 93–94). This conscription pattern sometimes had disadvantages from a military viewpoint, since it deprived new conscripts of the sense of solidarity and shared understandings characteristic of the old regional units. On the other hand, if a unit was to be used to repress civilian unrest, it was often useful for it to be ethnically and culturally different from the locality in which it operated.

14. H. Heller, *Staatslehre* (3d ed.; Leiden, 1963), pp. 109ff. This important book was first published in 1934 in a posthumous and incomplete edition. The author had died the year before, shortly after leaving Germany. On Heller see W. Schluchter, *Entscheidung für den sozialen Rechtsstaat* (Cologne, 1968).

15. Heller, *Staatslehre*, p. 203.

16. M. Weber, *Economy and Society* (Totowa, N.J., 1968), vol. 1, p. 65.

17. Heller, *Staatslehre*, p. 204.

18. N. Luhmann, *Macht* (Stuttgart, 1975), p. 103.

19. The significance of taxation as the chief means of financing the state's activities was emphasized by Hegel in par. 299 of his *Philosophy of Law*.

20. E. Durkheim, *Professional Ethics and Civic Morals* (London, 1957), p. 81.

21. Ferdinand Tönnies formulated this dichotomy in his greatest work, *Gemeinschaft und Gesellschaft* (1st ed., 1887), as a conceptual aid to the categorization of basic forms of social bond. For an English version, see S. Loomis, trans. and ed., *Community and Association* (East Lansing, Mich., 1957). Prototypical *Gemeinschaften* are a community of kin, a group of lifelong friends, the (idealized) medieval village—spontaneous, durable groupings encompassing the full individuality of their members and envisaging an open-ended plurality of shared interests. Prototypical *Gesellschaften* are a business partnership and a large-scale "formal" organization—groupings brought about artificially, for specific purposes, and affecting only differentiated segments of their members' existence. See the "Note on *Gemeinschaft* and *Gesellschaft*" in T. Parsons, *The Structure of Social Action* (New York, 1937), pp. 686–96. Most of Simmel's sociological characterizations of the modern state are compatible with my own statements about its "modernity." See for instance, G. Simmel, *Philosophie des Geldes* (6th ed.; Berlin, 1958), pp. 526–27.

22. Heller, *Staatslehre*, pp. 250–51.

23. M. Weber, "Religious Rejections of the World and Their Directions," in H. H. Gerth and C. W. Mills, trans. and eds., *From Max Weber: Essays in Sociology* (New York, 1958), pp. 323ff (esp. pp. 333–40).

24. Cited by Mommsen in *Max Weber und die deutsche Politik*, p. 216.

25. On the presuppositions and implications of this type of legiti-

macy, see N. Luhmann, *Legitimation durch Verfahren* (2d ed.; Neu-wied, 1975).

26. See N. Luhmann, *Rechtssoziologie* (Reinbek, 1972), vol. 2, pp. 207ff.

27. Heller, *Staatslehre*, p. 242.

28. J. Habermas, *Strukturwandel der Öffentlichkeit* (5th ed.; Neu-wied, 1971), p. 105.

29. I am focusing here on *one* functional aspect of the public rights of the citizenry—the defense against the dangers inherent in the open-ended and increasing state regulation of social affairs. But it should be borne in mind that such regulation was largely a response to the rapid erosion of the existing, chiefly customary and local rules for everyday conduct in the face of socioeconomic and cultural change. Accordingly, only a supralocal, rational mechanism for public decision-making could fill the resulting "anomic" vacuum by elaborating new, abstract, and flexible frameworks of regulation, which it then would enforce. From this perspective, the citizens' public rights appear not as barriers against the state's abuse of its regulatory powers, but as vital feedback devices for activating and steering the exercise of those powers on behalf of the civil society and its dominant components.

30. See C. Roehrssen, "Il diritto pubblico verso la 'teoria generale.' Georg Jellinek," in G. Tarello, ed., *Materiali per una storia della cultura giuridica*, vol. 6 (Bologna, 1976), pp. 291ff.

31. Jellinek, *Allgemeine Staatslehre*, p. 372.

32. C. Schmitt, *Legalität und Legitimität* (Munich, 1932).

33. Cited by Habermas in *Strukturwandel der Öffentlichkeit*, p. 144.

34. See, for example, Rochat, "L'esercito e il fascismo."

35. C. Schmitt, "Die Prinzipien des Parlamentarismus," in K. Kluxen, ed., *Parlamentarismus* (Cologne, 1967), pp. 41–53.

36. Again, this potential importance of parliament is a central pre-occupation in Max Weber's political thinking, as shown by Mommsen in *Max Weber und die deutsche Politik*.

CHAPTER VI

1. See, for example, *Democracy in America* (London, 1969), vol. 2, p. 698.

2. K. Marx, *Early Writings* (Harmondsworth, Eng., 1970), p. 181.

3. A. Gouldner, *The Coming Crisis of Western Sociology* (New York, 1970), pp. 304–13, gives an excellent statement of this point.

4. J. Habermas, *Strukturwandel der Öffentlichkeit* (5th ed.; Neuwied, 1971), pp. 74–75. My debt to this book (and to others of Habermas's

writings) is particularly considerable in the first few sections of this chapter. The reader might note, however, that some of Habermas's arguments have been controverted; see, for instance, W. Jäger, *Öffentlichkeit und Parlamentarismus: Eine Kritik an Jürgen Habermas* (Stuttgart, 1973).

5. "Though politics ideally stands above the power of money, it has in fact become money's bondsman." K. Marx, *Frühe Schriften* (Stuttgart, 1962), vol. 1, p. 483. For a general statement of this position, yet one emphasizing the extent to which the nature of the capitalist mode of production prohibits the direct conferral of public power on the capitalist class as such, see U. K. Preuss, *Bildung und Herrschaft* (Frankfurt, 1975), pp. 7–44.

6. For two differently derived statements of the societal supremacy of the economy and its distinctive interests, see the section on the "civil society" in G. W. F. Hegel, *Philosophy of Right* (Oxford, 1942), pp. 122ff.; and E. Troeltsch, *The Social Teachings of the Christian Churches* (New York, 1960), p. 28.

7. J. Habermas et al., *Student und Politik* (Neuwied, 1961), p. 23.

8. On the significance of this principle for the bourgeois-liberal polity, see L. Kofler, *Staat Gesellschaft und Elite Zwischen Humanismus und Nihilismus* (Ulm, 1960), pp. 126ff.

9. T. Geiger, *Saggi sulla società industriale* (Turin, 1970), pp. 613, 617f. This is the Italian translation of Geiger's *Demokratie ohne Dogma* (1964).

10. See A. Gouldner, *Dialectics of Ideology and Technology* (London, 1976), pp. 101f.

11. The argument here and below about "balanceable" versus "unbalanceable" interests, and about the impact of the latter's entry into politics, is based on W. Hofmann, "Staat und Politisches Handeln Heute," in his *Abschied vom Bürgertum* (Frankfurt, 1970), pp. 179ff. On the varying success of the subaltern strata, see R. Bendix, *Nation-Building and Citizenship* (New York, 1964), pp. 74ff.

12. See, for example, L. Charnay, *Société militaire et suffrage politique en France depuis 1789* (Paris, 1964).

13. See C. B. Macpherson, *The Real World of Democracy* (Oxford, 1966), pp. 8f.

14. For a sophisticated treatment of this and other aspects of the lower classes' entry into politics focused on a historically significant variant of this phenomenon, see G. Roth, *The Social Democrats in Imperial Germany* (Totowa, N.J., 1962).

15. See T. Lowi, *The End of Liberalism* (New York, 1969), chap. 4, for some American examples of this phenomenon and a critique of its consequences.

16. C. Offe, *Leistungsprinzip und industrielle Arbeit* (Frankfurt, 1970), p. 13.

17. Habermas, *Strukturwandel der Öffentlichkeit*, pp. 187f.

18. Lowi, *End of Liberalism*, p. 6. For a more technical statement of the "privileging" nature of such legal operations, see F. Galgano, *Storia del diritto commerciale* (Bologna, 1976), chaps. 3 and 6.

19. On some of these arrangements, see A. Schofield, *Modern Capitalism* (Oxford, 1966).

20. H. P. Bahrdt, *Die moderne Grosstadt* (Rowohlt, 1962), pp. 43f.

21. For a discussion of this phenomenon from the perspective of the sociology of law, see P. Selznick, *Law, Society and Industrial Justice* (New York, 1969).

22. See, for instance, J. O'Connor, *The Fiscal Crisis of the State* (New York, 1973).

23. E.-W. Böckenförde, "Die Bedeutung der Unterscheidung von Staat und Gesellschaft im demokratischen Sozialstaat der Gegenwart," in *Rechtsfragen der Gegenwart* (Stuttgart, 1972), pp. 11ff. (this passage at p. 28). V. Ronge and G. Schmieg, *Restriktionen politischer Planung* (Frankfurt, n.d.), can be seen as supporting Böckenförde's main argument from a different perspective while at the same time applying it to the uses of "planning" as a technique of political-administrative management.

24. See P. Saraceno, "Le radici della crisi economica," *Il Mulino* 25, no. 243 (Jan.–Feb. 1976): 3ff.

25. In this chapter, as elsewhere, I have purposely avoided any discussion of the considerable but currently somewhat overfashionable problem of the relation between national states, on the one hand, and multinational corporations and supranational organizations, on the other.

26. I borrow the expression "the web of rules" from C. Kerr et al., *Industrialism and Industrial Man* (London, 1962), p. 76.

27. A. Gehlen, *Studien zur Anthropologie und Soziologie* (Neuwied, 1963), p. 255.

28. See the significance attributed to political ceremonies and symbols in discussions of the role of communal rituals in contemporary society in R. Bellah, "Civil Religion in America," in his *Beyond Belief* (New York, 1970), pp. 168ff.

29. This follows from the very notion of "scope" as a component of

influence or power. See, for instance, H. Lasswell and A. Kaplan, *Power and Society* (New Haven, Conn., 1950), pp. 73, 77.

30. See A. Gouldner, "Metaphysical Pathos and the Theory of Democracy," in S. M. Lipset and N. Smelser, eds., *Sociology: The Progress of a Decade* (Englewood Cliffs, N.J., 1961), pp. 8off.

31. W. Niskanen, *Bureaucracy: Servant or Master?* (London, 1973), pp. 2off.

32. M. Crozier, *The Bureaucratic Phenomenon* (Chicago, 1964).

33. A. Görlitz, *Demokratie im Wandel* (Cologne, 1969), p. 84.

34. The significance of discussion for classical parliamentarism is much emphasized in C. Schmitt, "Die Prinzipien des Parlamentarismus," in K. Kluxen, ed., *Parlamentarismus* (Cologne, 1967), pp. 41ff.

35. On this point, the statement by R. Michels in *Political Parties* (London, 1915) remains fundamental.

36. See O. Kirchheimer, *Politics, Law and Social Change* (New York, 1969), pp. 245–371.

37. For the distinction between "conditional" and "target" programming of administrative action, rephrased here, see N. Luhmann, "Opportunismus und Programmatik in der öffentlichen Verwaltung," in his *Politische Planung* (Opladen, 1971), pp. 165ff.

38. See R. Mayntz and F. Scharpf, eds., *Planungsorganisation* (Munich, 1973), chap. 4.

39. The thesis that it is the paradoxical particularity of the West to have its distinctive cultural achievements acquire universal significance is stated in the opening sentences of the "Einleitung" to M. Weber, *Gesammelte Aufsätze zur Religionssoziologie*, vol. 1 (Tübingen, 1920), pp. 1–5.

40. See for instance N. Matteucci, *Il liberalismo in un mondo in transformazione* (Bologna, 1972); and K. O. Hondrich, *Theorie der Herrschaft* (Frankfurt, 1975).

41. For a vigorous contemporary restatement of the political inadequacies of the socialist, and particularly the Marxist, traditions, see N. Bobbio, *Quale socialismo?* (Turin, 1976). On the troubled relations between the socialist and the democratic traditions, see A. Rosenberg, *Demokratie und Sozialismus* (Frankfurt, 1964).

42. R. M. Unger's *Knowledge and Politics* (New York, 1975) is distinguished among other things by the combination of learning, lucidity, and passion with which it criticizes the liberal tradition and seeks to project a radically new understanding of the present political predicament of the West that will also transcend some of the assumptions and limitations of democratic theory.

Index

Abstractness of laws, 73, 84, 86, 97, 143f
Administrative arrangements: in the Ständestaat, 54; in the absolutist system, 70–71, 72, 77, 83; in Prussia, 74–77; in the constitutional state, 94, 98; in the contemporary state, 136–38, 143–44. *See also* Bureaucracy; Public law
Administrative law, 87
Administrative personnel: in the absolutist system, 70–71, 75f; in the constitutional state, 94, 109; in the contemporary state, 136–38. *See also* Bureaucracy
Alliances: among towns, 38, 41; for peace, 55
Allocation: and the nature of politics, 2–5, 6, 11f, 92; and the state, 119, 125, 138
Allodium, 23, 29
Ancien régime, 18, 81, 85, 111
Anderson, Perry, 155, 162
Armed conflict, 7–8, 10
Army: in the feudal system, 22, 66; in the absolutist system, 53–54, 66, 70; in Prussia, 74; in the constitutional state, 94, 108, 110, 113. *See also* Conscription; Military arrangements; War
Artificiality of the state, 95f, 98–99

Bahrdt, Hans: quoted, 128
Ban, 26–27
Bargaining, 124, 137
Beneficium, 20–22. *See also* Fief
Bishops, *see* Clergy
Bismarck, Otto von, 89
Böckenförde, Ernst-Wolfgang, 58, 132, 134; quoted, 130–31
Boundaries, 90, 93
Bourbon dynasty, 138
Bourgeoisie, 125–27; in the absolutist system, 62, 65f, 79–81, 83, 162; entrepreneurial element in, 64f, 79–80, 109; as estate in the Ständestaat, 78; as class, 78–80, 83, 119; as public, 81ff, 84; intellectual and professional element in, 81–83, 123; in the constitutional state, 91, 119
Budget, 137, 143
Bullion, 61, 65, 78, 116
Bureaucracy, 74–77, 87, 136–38, 142

Canon law, 33, 57
Capital accumulation, xi, 81, 115ff, 119, 122, 126
Capitalism, 84, 120, 122, 125, 131; in the absolutist system, 61–64, 79; in the constitutional state, 94–95, 114, 120f; and capitalist mode of production, 108–9, 115f, 117–21 *passim*, 123, 129, 134; in the con-